Audacious American Women

Emily Pritchard Cary

Audacious American Women

Copyright 2012 by Emily Pritchard Cary. All rights reserved.

Published by Matthew Mylles

Audacious American Women

Other books by Emily Cary:

My High Love Calling

The Ghost of Whitaker Mountain

Duet: Melodrama in Three-Quarter Time

The Pritchard Family History from Thomas of Jamestown

The Treasure of Juniper Junction

The Loudoun Legacy

Peril in Patagonia

The Pembroke Path

Audacious American Women

Dedication

To my sons, Roger and Roland

Audacious American Women

Table of Contents

Preface	1
The Women of Deerfield	3
Salome Weidner Atkinson	28
Margaret Forster Steuart	61
Rose O'Neal Greenbow	81
Lydia Knapp Horton	125
Women of Arizona Territorial Asylum	157
Lily Belle Kellogg Hancock	186
Grace Voss Frederick	216
Florence Jenkins Muse	236

Audacious American Women

Audacious American Women

Preface

History has given us many audacious women, women who defied authority and society's expectations to trample barriers in order to better their lives and those of others. Jeanne d'Arc, Molly Brown, Amelia Earhart, Harriet Tubman, and Susan B. Anthony are familiar names to most, but there are legions of women known only to their families or communities. Their ordeals leading sometimes to success, often to failure, are recorded in obscure documents buried in archives or family trunks.

Until modern times, women of the Western world were

traditionally governed and their freewheeling ambitions squelched by men, perhaps fathers, husbands, lovers, religious fanatics, or rulers. How exciting to live during an era in which women have risen to the top in politics, business, and the clergy because they are the best qualified candidates.

Some of the women celebrated within these pages might have known different endings had they been born later. Still, they and their feisty sisters who have withstood strife, hardships, widowhood, and prejudices left behind messages of hope and encouragement for future generations of women.

THE WOMEN OF DEERFIELD:
ABIGAIL MARGUERITE STEBBINS
EUNICE WILLIAMS

Abigail Marguerite Stebbins was born at Deerfield, Massachusetts on January 4, 1683/84, the eldest of seven children of Captain John Stebbins Jr. and Dorothy Alexander. She, her siblings, and a young neighbor were destined to play major roles in the infamous Deerfield Massacre of February 1704.

Captain Stebbins, the eldest son of Deacon John Stebbins and Mary Ann Munson, was the first of his line born in the

Massachusetts Colony. His father, John Sr., was only eight years old when he boarded the ship "Francis" at Ipswich, Suffolk County, England on the last day of April 1634. The youngest son of Rowland and Sarah Stebbins, John Sr., along with his parents and his three siblings (Thomas, 14, Sarah, 11, and Elizabeth, 6), had joined the Puritan emigration to New England. They left behind in numerous Parish Registers of Essex, Suffolk and London extensive family records tracing back to the arrival of their French ancestor with the Norman invasion at the Battle of Hastings in 1066.

The Rowland Stebbins family, residents of the parish of Bocking near Braintree, England, may have been inspired to emigrate to the colonies after listening to sermons by Thomas Hooker, the future founder of Hartford, Connecticut. But instead of following Hooker and other neighbors to Connecticut, they chose to first settle in Roxbury, Massachusetts founded by William Pynchon, the father of Rowland's close friend Captain John Pynchon. Later, the Stebbins family moved to Northampton, Hampshire County, Massachusetts where both

Rowland and his son John died, Roland on December 14, 1671 and John on March 07, 1677/78.

    Deacon John Stebbins was only 20 when he bought land in Springfield, Massachusetts and built a house, but by 1656 he had moved on to Northampton where he lived at the lower end of "Pudding Lane," later renamed Hawley Street. He owned a sawmill in Easthampton and was an active member of the community. In 1659 and 1671, he was assigned as a surveyor of lands and in 1684 was elected town bailiff. His job entailed clearing the meadows of all cattle and swine that did not belong there in order to prevent destruction of corn crops and grass. He was elected as a selectman in 1675 and again in 1678, the year he died at his sawmill.

    Although the cause of his death was an accident, superstition ran rampant throughout the colony. Consequently, his death was presented to the court as the result of witchcraft. Half of the jurors believed this to be the case, so an inquest was held. During the process, his body was examined twice and many women were commanded to appear at court and touch him. It was believed that the culprit would be revealed during this procedure, but no visible miracles transpired and he eventually was buried without concrete proof that a witch had been at fault.

Deacon John and Mary Stebbins had sixteen children. The eldest, Captain John Stebbins Jr., was born January 28, 1646/47 in Springfield, Hampden County, Massachusetts. As a youth, he managed to find trouble, first when he was not yet 20 for complicity in a burglary with his half-brother Benoni and a friend, Godfrey Nims. While the townspeople were in church, the young men stole twelve shillings of silver and seven of wampum. They later explained that they committed the crime because Quanquelatt, a local Indian, encouraged them to steal the money as payment for his promise to help them run away to Canada.

All four were found guilty of the crime and sentenced to lashes on their bare backs. Quanquelatt received twenty lashes and John, the ringleader, was to receive fifteen, while Benoni and Godfrey were each to be given eleven. At the last minute, the boys received a reprieve when John's father paid a forty-shilling fine. Quanquelatt was the only one to pay the painful price. Thus, the anticipated flight to Canada did not come to pass at that time, but one suspects that young John was not yet repentant, for in 1674 he was accused by five people of "lascivious carriage."

Although the outcome of this latter case eludes local records, John Stebbins Jr. may have been required to serve time in the militia as penance, for he was serving at Springfield under Captain Lathrop at the outset of King Philip's War. That conflict, regarded as the first of the French and Indian wars, found the Indians and their French supporters fighting the colonists. It lasted from 1675 to 1678 and was named after Metacomet, an Indian chief whom the British called King Philip.

On September 18, 1675, the war took a violent turn with the Bloody Brook Massacre in Deerfield. Stebbins was the only survivor who was not wounded. Apparently the experience was sufficient chastisement to impress him with the folly of his ways. The very next day, he enlisted under Captain Samuel Mosely and continued to serve until the close of the war. After taking the oath of Allegiance in Northampton on February 8, 1678, he made his home near Boston. Four years passed before he moved to lot

35 in the permanent settlement at Deerfield.

Following the Bloody Brook ambush on Deerfield, the militia made a surprise raid on the nearby Indian camp and killed more than 300, including women and children. Prudently, the English settlers avoided the area for a number of years until the village was surrounded by a stockade inside a palisade fence. A few hired soldiers provided added protection. Once their safety was assured by this arrangement, Stebbins and other families moved in. They farmed the rich soil of this frontier land and felt relatively secure from attacks by the French and nearby Indians. Nevertheless, they always kept their trusty pistols ready for an emergency; even the women and youngsters knew how to handle a musket.

Two decades after overcoming his wild youth, John Stebbins Jr. held several offices in the village and enjoyed a relatively settled life as a family man. With the onset of winter and farm chores slumbering until spring, he and the other townspeople never anticipated the surprise raid on February 29, 1704. Most were still asleep in their beds on that bitterly cold morning when Mohawk Indians besieged the village. Houses were set afire and many inhabitants trying to hide in their root cellars burned to death.

Those who resisted were killed instantly by hatchet, gunshot, knife, or war club. Their bloody bodies lay in the new-fallen snow. Only a fortunate few escaped with minor wounds. Of the 300 original residents of Deerfield, 133 managed to hide during the battle or flee the attackers. Another 109 survivors were not so fortunate. They were taken hostage and marched away by the Indians and French militia who had launched the expedition.

The purpose of the raid was to discourage the English colonists from settling on lands previously utilized by France for their lucrative fur trade. Years earlier, the French had formed alliances with Indian tribes across North America to protect both the fur trade and the native habitat. In contrast, the English were greedy and developed a reputation for grabbing Indian lands and fighting the natives who lived there. For this reason, the French and Indians banded together to oppose English settlements.

While historians do not know specifically what prompted the raid on Deerfield, it was likely an accumulation of cruel actions by the English. The Indians probably sought revenge for the killing of many Mohawk women and children by the militia. As for the French, they profited by the taking of captives. Because the Jesuit missionaries who accompanied the earliest French trappers to Canada were very successful in converting many Indians to Catholicism, all captives were potential Catholics who enabled the church to grow and prosper.

Despite valiant efforts by local militiaman to save those captured at Deerfield, the French and Indians wounded so many pursuers that they were driven back and compelled to halt the chase. The Stebbins home was among those burned down. Although no members were injured, the entire family was taken hostage.

Stebbins, his wife Dorothy, and their children were one of the few families who survived the long walk to Montreal, Canada. Many of their 109 fellow captives died or were killed along the way. Throughout the journey, the eldest Stebbins daughter, Abigail Marguerite, then 20, and her husband, Jacques De Noyen, helped tend to the needs of her siblings Samuel, 16; Thankful, 13; Ebenezer, 10; Mary Elizabeth, 6; and Joseph, 5.

The march was long and treacherous. There were steep mountains to climb and waterways to cross or avoid by traveling many additional miles. Snow lay deep on the ground. The thick underbrush delayed progress, and a layer of ice covered the streams. Some of the captives managed to wade across the shallow rivers, while others fell in and drowned. The clothes of many were so soaked that pneumonia felled them before long.

After a trek of eight days with little sleep, they reached the junction of the Connecticut and White Rivers, then proceeded north through the Green Mountains to Lake Champlain. There they traveled up the lake by walking on the thick ice. Throughout the journey, their food was limited to dried moose flesh, nuts, and cranberries.

On April 15, 1704, nearly six weeks after the Deerfield Massacre, they reached the French fort at Chambly. It was manned by French officers who had been responsible for the attack. After confirming the identity and physical condition of each captive, they sent them on, by way of Iroquois villages, to Montreal, where they were indoctrinated in Catholicism by the Jesuits. This was against the beliefs of the Puritans, who regarded that religion as "Popery." Indeed, many had sailed to the colonies to escape the influence of that church. While the Reverend John Williams and others in his company successfully resisted conversion, the younger adults and children accepted the faith without protest.

As the months passed, the captives and their captors developed close relationships. These relationships were further complicated by the strong presence of French Catholicism in their daily lives and the mingling of the French, English, and Indian languages. The intermarriage that often followed became the deciding factor for many captives to stay in Canada and follow the French way of life there.

Eunice Williams, the daughter of Reverend Williams, was only seven years old the day she awoke to the violent attack.

Despite the cruel hardships endured by others on the trek, even the murder of her own mother when the poor woman could walk no longer, she was treated well and was carried most of the way on the shoulders of the Mohawk warriors who captured her. Upon her arrival at Kahnawake, the great Indian city of longhouses, Eunice was welcomed by the women. They adopted her into the community, even as her father was sent on to Montreal.

Eunice soon became one of them, learning to plant, cultivate and harvest the crops, prepare the deer killed by hunting parties, and master the catechism taught by the nearby Jesuits. Soon the Mohawk and French languages became second nature to her and she forgot the English she had learned as a child. At a midwinter festival, she took her new name, Marguerite Kanenstenhawi. Now she was a Mohawk.

At age 16, she married Arosen, a Mohawk warrior who adopted Catholicism and took the name François Xavier as his Christian name. Despite Reverend Williams' ultimate release from captivity and his numerous attempts to reunite with his daughter, she chose to remain with her adopted Indian family of the Wôbanakiak tribe. Even though the Jesuits encouraged her to return to her English roots, she and Arosen declined. They had at least two daughters who lived to old age and may have had a son because Reverend Williams often spoke of his grandson, but proof does not exist because many records were destroyed by fire.

Over the years, Eunice Marguerite and her husband visited the Williams family in Massachusetts. Although she remained illiterate, she continued to communicate with her brother Stephen through emissaries until his death in 1782. She died three years later at age 89, but her grandchildren often visited Stephen's grandchildren.

Abigail Stebbins had been married less than a month when French Captain de Rouville took command of the entire family in the march through deep snows and the ice of Lake Champlain to the French fort at Chambly, New France. Fortune may have been on the side of the family, for Abigail's husband was Sergeant Jacques Rene De Noyon, a native of Trois-Rivieres, Quebec. It is likely that the Stebbins family was spared death because of his presence and congenial conversations with Captain de Roubille along the way.

Amiable though he was at first glance, De Noyon was an adventurer capable of undertaking questionable exploits and twisting the truth. At the age of 20, he and three companions traveled to the Canadian West where they discovered the Lake of the Woods in Winnipeg and spent the winter of 1688-89 exploring the area. The record of De Noyon's westward adventures is contained in a narrative he wrote that is cited in various documents. It includes an account of the trading party he led to Rainy Lake, in what is today Minnesota, where they wintered among the Assiniboine tribe, relatives of the Sioux. At that time, he had journeyed further west than any known Frenchman. During his trip home in 1689, a member of his company named Lacroix was accidentally drowned in a lake that was later called Lac Saint-Croix.

De Noyon's varied adventures were often dangerous. In

1690, he was hired by Francois Charon de La Barre to travel west and collect a debt from one Gilles Papin. The venture took him to the Michigan peninsula as guide to a party of travelers. Each year he regularly earned 200 livres (the French form of currency until 1795, roughly equivalent to the British pound) for collecting debts, but when he met up with Papin at the start of the new year in 1698, he was slightly drunk. Before collecting the debt, he managed to insult Papin. In response, Papin drew his sword. De Noyon escaped with nothing but a ruined reputation. As his credit dissolved, he accumulated enormous debts.

His promise to obtain furs for another venture also ended in failure. At that point, he was stranded in Deerfield and decided to settle there to assess his situation. It was not long before his claims to be well established and wealthy attracted the trusting residents and he soon began courting Abigail Stebbins, One envisions her as a charming young lady whose beauty must have captured De Noyon's fancy sufficiently for him to consider marriage for the first time in his adventurous life. They were married in Deerfield on February 3, 1703-04 by Reverend John

Williams, little suspecting that their lives would soon take a nasty turn and they would become fellow captives.

During the long trek to Canada, Abigail fared better than most of the women in the hapless group. Thanks to his ancestry and imposing personality, De Noyon was able to convince the French officers of his trustworthiness. His young bride was greatly impressed by his ability to charm the officers and ease their situation. Even though her parents and oldest brother remained prisoners, Abigail and her husband were released and allowed to take her brothers Ebenezer and Joseph and her sister, Mary Elizabeth, with them to Montreal. They all moved into the home of De Noyon's widowed mother in nearby Boucherville. Abigail had no way of knowing that she was destined to spend the rest of her life there.

Their first of their fifteen children was born December 26, 1704 and baptized two days later. Even though she had been raised as a Puritan, an enemy of Catholicism, Abigail reluctantly joined the Catholic church to please her husband. She herself was baptized at Notre-Dame Montreal on May 28, 1708 in the presence of sponsors Philippe de Rigaud Vaudreuil, Governor of Canada, and Marguerite Bonat Pascaud, the wife of one of Vaudreuil's generals. At her baptism, Abigail changed her name to Marie Gabrielle, and was known as Gabrielle by her family from that moment on.

Abigail's siblings remained in her charge and converted to the Catholic faith, as she had done. Ebenezer had been 10 years old when captured. On June 19, 1708, he was baptized at Chambly as Jacques Charles Stebenne. In 1714, he was naturalized as a Canadian and probably remained there the rest of his life, although he is thought to have returned to New England to visit with his family some time after 1731.

Abigail's youngest brother, Joseph, was only five when he was captured. Initially, he accompanied his sister to her husband's home, but he was later adopted by the wealthy De Rouville family and moved in prestigious circles because of that connection. Like Ebenezer, he changed the spelling of his surname to the French Stebenne and remained in Quebec until his death on 23 April 1753 in St. Mathais, Rouville, Chambly.

He married Marie-Marguerite Sanssouci on November 18, 1734 in Fort Chambly. One of the witnesses to the marriage was Sieur de Niverville, then commander of the fort. The marriage contract was drawn up by Father LeVassaeur, curate for the King. Joseph never returned to America and raised his family of nine in Quebec. He is responsible for founding the prolific Stebenne family of Canada.

Mary Elizabeth Stebbins, Abigail's youngest sister, was five at the time of capture. After journeying to Boucherville with her sister, she remained there until 29 July 1715 when she married Joseph Jonace Raizenne at Lac Des Montagnes. No records have been located confirming that she ever returned to visit her family in Deerfield.

When she first met De Noyon, Abigail was charmed by his ways and his claims to wealth. Once she had settled in Quebec, she discovered how greatly his stories were exaggerated. Upon their arrival in Quebec, De Noyon was dunned for unpaid bills. As the truth unfolded, Abigail realized that she was trapped with a less than honorable man in a strange country at war with hers. With no visible support, she had little recourse. To provide for herself and her children, she was compelled to do manual labor and to accept charity.

In a petition she made on July 9, 1708 to Pierre Reimbault, Esquire, the King's counselor and attorney in Canada, she prayed that the joint estate she held with her husband be dissolved and that she be authorized to buy in her own name a farm in Boucherville. The petition and subsequent deeds referred to her as "Marguerite Stebens."

In the petition, she claimed that her husband was heavily in debt and provided her no financial help whatsoever. She expressed hope of supporting herself and her children from the farm produce and paying off the purchase price by a combination of her own efforts and help she expected from her parents once the war ended. The petition was approved and she finally was able to fend for herself.

At that time, De Noyon was a sergeant in the marine troops in the company of Captain de Tonty. He held the highest non-commissioned rank with a decent monthly salary. It was not an ample sum, however, for supporting a family and repaying his multiple debts. In 1708, his entire fortune was less than 400 livres. To manage their household, Abigail was compelled to seek charity. Meanwhile, her husband would continue his travels in various capacities, although he found time to return home long enough to reproduce nearly one offspring per year until 1725.

While Abigail first settled at Boucherville, Quebec and was finding survival extremely difficult, her father John Stebbins Jr., her mother Dorothy, and her oldest brother, John III, were held in Chambly. Through efforts by their English friends, they eventually were ransomed and returned to Deerfield, where their first task was to build a home to replace the one burned to the ground during the raid.

Samuel Stebbins, who was 18 years old at the time of his capture, was separated from the family at the outset of the march and was thought for many years to have died. However, they must have had some word from him over time because his father's will written July 31, 1723 indicated that Samuel was still in Canada. Subsequently, he returned to Deerfield prior to 1731. It is not known if he remained in Massachusetts or went back to Canada.

    Thankful Stebbins, thirteen years old at the time of her capture, was kept by Captain de Rouville at his home in Chambly. At her baptism on 23 April 1707, she was given the name of Louise Therese. Her godparents were Squire Rene Hertel de Roubville and Madame de Perigny, wife of the commander of Fort Chambly. She grew up amid a genteel society of French army officers and their wives. In 1711 at the age of 19, she married Adrien Charles Legrain, dit Lavelee, a militia captain. Her sister Abigail, entered into the record of the event as Marguerite Steben, was in attendance with Jacques De Noyon. Thankful and her husband had nine children. The youngest, Veronique, was born just one week before Thankful's death in Chambly on July 11, 1729 at the age of 37. Her husband survived another nineteen years.

In 1714, after the war was resolved, Abigail managed to send her oldest son, Jacques Rene De Noyon, then ten years old, to live with her parents in Deerfield. He remained with them and changed his name to Aaron Denio. In December 1753, he settled in Greenfield, Hampshire County, Massachusetts leaving many descendants whose surname spelling has evolved to Danio.

If Abigail had contact with her family, one wonders why she remained in Quebec with a husband who provided scant support and a life of drudgery. No doubt she was guided by the teachings of the Catholic church and the conviction that she must bear the burdens required of life. It is easy to envision the young woman gradually failing in appearance and health during her struggles with the soil and a household of children to manage.

She withstood the rigorous life until the age of 56 when she died, leaving a husband then in his mid-seventies. Too old and weary to work the land that Abigail had cultivated throughout their marriage, De Noyon willed all his resources to his children on 26 April 1742, then moved in with his daughter Marie and son-in-law Louis Renaud. Until his death three years later, he remained there supported by a 200 livre life annuity from his children.

Stebbins House, Deerfield, Massachusetts as it looks today. It was rebuilt by the family after the Raid.

Credit: Deerfield, Massachusetts Historical Museum

REFERENCES

Churchyard, James Nohl, The French and Indian Raid on Deerfield, Massachusetts, 1704.

Dictionaire Genealogique Des Families Canadiennes, Volume VII, pp. 219, 558.

French Canadian & Acadian Genealogical review, Vol., III, Spring 1971.

Frenier, J. Henry, Canadian Branch of the Stebbins Family.

Greenlee, Ralph Stebbins and Robert Lemuel Greenlee, The Stebbins Genealogy, Volume I, 1904.

http://Tufts.journal.tufts.edu/archive/2004/January/features/Deerfield-raid.

http://www.geocities.com/ve6xv/KingPhilip.html.

http://nationalreview.com/comment/miller_molesky20041004.

Melvoin, Richard I., New England Outpost, 1988, pp. 83, 138.

Russ, C. J., Canadian Biographies

Sheldon, George, A History of Deerfield Massachusetts, New Hampshire Publishing Company, 1972.

Stebbins, Willis Merrill, Genealogy of the Stebbins Family and Kindred Lines), Gothenburg, New Brunswick, 1940.

Stebbins Family Genealogy, line from Bocking, England to Emily Pritchard Cary.

www.1704.deerfield.history.com

www.americanheritage.com/acticles/magazine/ah.1993.

SALOME WEIDNER ATKINSON

January 7, 1755-March 25, 1809

During her lifetime, Salome Weidner Atkinson played many roles, among them daughter, wife, mother, teacher, temptress, and progenitor of famous Americans. Her story begins at Ephrata Cloister on Cocalico Creek in Lancaster County, Pennsylvania, where a gene pool mix sired a line of brilliant achievers, extraordinarily beautiful women, and movers and shakers of early Pennsylvania society.

Ephrata Cloister was founded in 1732 by Johann Conrad

Beissel, a German religious eccentric, mystic, and strict disciplinarian. Despite his promotion of celibacy as the true way to salvation, several followers strayed from that rule. The resulting mix precipitated a medical breakthrough five generations later. But wait! Events in the interim bear explanation.

Early in the 18th century, Pennsylvania already was becoming a melting pot of religious thinkers. Fervent beliefs propelled at least half of its early colonists across the ocean. William Penn ferried Quakers from England, Welsh Baptists fled the King's men to the Welsh Colony outside Philadelphia, and German and Swiss immigrants sought freedom to worship freely as Lutherans, Moravians, and Mennonites. Smaller sects like Beissel's began cropping up west of Philadelphia as early as 1711 when the Pietists settled in the Berks County village of Oley.

They were joined there in 1718 by the zealous New Borns (Die Neugeborne) founded by Matthias Bauman, a laborer from the Lower Palatinate. His religious conversion was in response to the vision he saw while in a trance that lasted several weeks. Many Germans and Swiss settled in Germantown just outside Philadelphia. Like the Quakers, they gradually made their way into the wilderness, drawn by men like Beissel who advocated close communities centered around their beliefs.

Several families destined to unite in later generations, were already in place when Beissel established his settlement. About 1700, Thomas Atkinson arrived in Philadelphia with his infant son, Stephen, and other English Quakers sailing under the auspices of William Penn. By 1730, Stephen had purchased a farm on the Conestoga River in Lancaster County. In typical Quaker fashion, he raised eight well educated children, all trained in useful professions. His fourth son, Thomas, born in 1751, studied architecture and masonry, trades that would prove profitable in the growing communities.

Before the autumn of 1724, Johannes Heinrich Schneider, a cordwainer (maker of fine shoes), emigrated from Germany with his son Frederick, daughter Catherine, her husband Peter Weidner, and their children. After the death on August 18, 1725 of Johannes (identified as Henry Snider in Will Book E:8 of Philadelphia County, Pennsylvania), Peter and Catherine Weidner moved to the Oley Valley.

    John Gorgas had emigrated to Philadelphia from Holland in 1708. A clockmaker, he anticipated great need for his craft by the newcomers and quickly established a business that would be regarded as the finest in the country for the next four generations. Not long after landing, he married Sytje (Psyche) Rittenhouse, whose parents had arrived from Holland prior to her birth in 1693. They settled in Germantown and soon began a family. Their fifth son, Jacob, born August 9, 1728, married Christina Mack, granddaughter of Brethren Church founder Alexander Mack. By 1763, Jacob Gorgas had settled in the town of Ephrata. There he passed along the skills learned from his father, teaching his son and grandson to construct grandfather clocks that remain valuable to this day.

    Bernhard and Elisabetha Lorentz Gitter, emigrants from the Palatinate, first settled in Somerset County, New Jersey as members of the Amwell religious community. Their daughter,

Susanna, was baptized on February 7, 1725 at the Somerville Reformed Church.

 Fate was about to unite these families. We will never know if they were drawn to the Ephrata Cloister by divine revelations, by the preaching of Johann Conrad Beissel, or by a personal desire for perfection. Perhaps it was their common language still spoken by the Pennsylvania Amish. We do know that Peter and Catherine Weidner/Widener and their son, Peter, Jr., became part of the community in 1736. Two years later, the Gitter family left the Amwell group in New Jersey and moved to Ephrata Cloister.

The Ephrata Cloister was by 1740 a large complex consisting of a meeting house, printing office, bake house, school house, various small buildings, and separate dormitories with individual cells for the single brethren and sisters. All men wore the habit of the Capuchins, or White Friars. It consisted of a shirt, trousers, and vest, with a long white gown and cowl made of woolen for the winter months and linen in summer. Except for petticoats instead of trousers, women dressed the same. All were given monastic names.

Beissel's Sabbatarian brotherhood required considerable discipline and personal restraints from the thirty-six brethren and thirty-five sisters living together. Each day, he read aloud confessions from the members detailing their sins. Strict celibacy, the ideal, was not mandatory for married couples. Young love, however, was frowned upon.

Contrary to the rules, Peter Weidner, Jr. and Susanna Gitter succumbed to human nature and fell in love. Their attraction became so strong that they rejected the celibacy clause in late 1747 or 1748 and asked Conrad Beissel for permission to marry. According to the group's official history, the wedding ceremony proceeded uneventfully until Beissel and his brother "took leave of the bridegroom with a kiss…and thus weakened the conjugal love between (the bride and groom)…so much that they could not embrace each other for eight days…Much agonizing transpired, during which Peter Weidner requested and received from both Beissel and Susanna, an annulment; she, however, had a change of heart, and successfully petitioned the courts to enforce her marriage."

Susanna realized that the only hope for the couple to save their marriage was to leave Ephrata Cloister and Beissel's influence immediately. Once they made that break, their situation improved. They settled in Cumru Township, Berks County where, over the years, they obtained considerable property and had three daughters, Sophia, Salome, and Mary. Salome was born January 7, 1755, four years before her father's sudden death.

What might have been a tragedy for another widow proved fortuitous for the uncommonly attractive Susanna Widener. From a large and promising field of suitors, she chose attorney James Whitehead, a strong proponent of formal education for women, whose loving tutelage opened unexpected doors for her daughters. Whitehead and his new family were all baptized at St. Gabriel's Church (then Lutheran) in Amity Township in 1764, James on April 15, and Sophia, Salome, and Mary on June 10. Susanna and James Whitehead then had two children of their own, Penelope and Elizabeth.

For better or worse, all five of Susanna's daughters inherited her stunning beauty and quickly became renowned for their good looks and intelligence. Sophia, the oldest, was the first to become embroiled in romance. She was only fourteen when John Boone, a cousin of Daniel, became enamored with her. In 1765, their first child was born out of wedlock.

Headstrong like her mother, Sophia defied tradition and local gossips and waited two years before agreeing to marry Boone. Soon after the birth of their third child, Boone died accidentally while working as a tanner. Barely a month passed after his death in March 1773 before the beauteous Sophia caught the fancy of John Biddle, the Surveyor General of Pennsylvania. They were married that October.

Despite his esteemed background and connections. Biddle proved to be a scoundrel. Accused of adulterating the flour used by the troops at the Battle of Brandywine, he fled to Nova Scotia under Governor Mifflin's threat to hang him from the nearest oak tree.

Meanwhile, Mary Widener married David Clymer, a son of George Clymer, a signer of the Declaration of Independence. Clymer, a lawyer, is described in a letter written by family members as "a man of bad character, but of high standing and great wealth."

Salome determined to do better. Her father had left her extensive property in Sinking Springs, a thousand acres of the most valuable land hear Reading. Although he had died when she was only four years old, Salome did not have a fatherless childhood for long. Her mother's marriage to Whitehead provided her with ample love, an elegant home and a rich education that would serve Salome well in the years to come.

Armed with a penchant for learning and the wildness attributed to her namesake, she was immediately drawn to a young architect newly arrived in town. She often recalled her first meeting with the young mason whose assignments throughout Reading had brought him to the attention of her stepfather. Whitehead was so impressed by the young man's work that he invited him home to meet his stepdaughter.

Thomas Atkinson was described by those who knew him as "eminently prepossessing." He, in turn, was captivated by Salome's beauty. It did not hurt that Peter Widener left her 1,000 acres of the most valuable land near Reading. At their very first meeting, Salome and Thomas fell hopeless in love. Whitehead congratulated himself for engineering the match. Salome was only seventeen when she married the talented, dashing Thomas Atkinson in 1772. They lived in Reading for several years while Thomas served time as a second lieutenant in the Revolutionary army. His service took him directly into the thick of the Battle of Brandywine.

During the war, their farm team was forcibly impressed into service by the government. It was used until after the Battle of Yorktown. Thomas and Salome expected their horses to be returned; instead, the team was totally ruined and no compensation was ever offered. During this period, Thomas and Salome had three children, daughters Elizabeth and Sophia, and son Peter, who died in childhood.

Upon learning they would have to replace their horses, a formidable expense, they decided to strike out in a new direction. The westward movement had begun in earnest. People were moving across Pennsylvania by the hundreds daily, and all were in need of lodging along the way. It seemed an ideal time to open a public house to serve these travelers.

Thomas and Salome decided to stake their venture by selling the Sinking Springs property she had inherited from her father. The buyer was General Mifflin, who later became a governor of Pennsylvania. The sale profit of $1,000 proved to be little more than worthless continental money. Undaunted, they managed to open a public hotel on a heavily traveled route in Silver Springs, Cumberland County, not far from Mechanicsburg. Thomas put his masonry skills to work throughout the area.

After four years, they grew tired of the constant petty demands made of an innkeeper and his wife. Then they heard about available land on the state road from Carlisle to Sunbury at the mouth of Raccoon Creek and decided it would be an ideal spot to farm. So they turned over the profitable public house to another enterprising family and moved to their new home.

Their two sons were born at the farm, first Thomas Jr. on July 11, 1781, then Mathew. It was a fine place to raise children, and other new families moving into the area brought a great deal of business to Thomas Sr. As his masonry business prospered, his desire to spread his wings surged. When word filtered back about the fertile farm lands and influx of families into the Thomas Creek Valley of Maryland, he could not resist. With Salome's approval, he disposed of the farm and moved his young family to Maryland.

There his reputation for outstanding work grew. Many of the sturdy stone farmhouses standing there today are the fruits of his labor. His fame spread, and within four years, he was summoned to Baltimore, moving the family onto the estate of George Lux. (A main street named for his honor in the city was later translated from the Latin spelling and is today known as Light Street.) A distant relative of Salome's, Lux was subsequently instrumental in persuading city officials to consider

Thomas for one phase of the Court House construction. They needed little urging, selecting Thomas over many other applicants.

The Baltimore Court House was a unique building, designed to stand on pillars so that the public street might run beneath it. Thomas Atkinson's portion of the prestigious contract involved placing the pillars and excavating the passageway for the street beneath.

Soon after he commenced work on the Court House, Atkinson became ill. The malady proved to be yellow fever, a common, and dreaded, disease of the times. At that point in history, nobody knew it was caused by mosquitoes. The fever wracked his body for three months. Because he knew that he must complete his portion of the Court House within the time specified in order that other contractors could begin their work, he decided to hire others, or sub-contract, to fulfill his job.

Atkinson was afraid that his failure to do the actual work himself would be a detriment to his career, but he planned so well and the men he hired carried out his assignments so successfully that the job brought him offers of more work than he had ever dreamed.

His reward was a commission to build the jail and market place in Alexandria, Virginia, a great honor for a young mason. While working on this contract over a period of five years, Atkinson moved his family to Alexandria. Toward the end of this period, he began to have a relapse; the yellow fever had taken hold once again.

Salome suggested that he curtail his masonry jobs and take a nice long rest in the country. Once the jail and market place were nearing completion, Atkinson agreed that her idea had merit, so he sought out a sprawling farm in Loudoun County, about twenty-three miles west of Alexandria.

It was a lovely, restful spot. Salome was relieved that her husband would have time to regain his strength. Their children, now totaling seven in number, were delighted with the country life. Like Salome, they fully expected their father to recuperate and be as good as new within weeks.

But as the summer of 1792 wore on, it became apparent

that the illness was stubborn. After deep discussion, Thomas and Salome concluded that the climate of Virginia was the culprit. Even though they hated to leave Virginia, it seemed wise to return to Pennsylvania where they never had been ill and where yellow fever was not nearly so common.

Thomas could not leave until seeing his masonry contracts to completion, an estimated two or three months away. And so he decided that Salome and the children should begin the trip back to Pennsylvania before the weather became severe. They would stay with relatives in Lancaster County until he arrived. There they could establish a new home of their own. He was certain that his reputation as a master mason throughout Maryland and Virginia would stand him in good stead for future assignments in Pennsylvania. It was only a matter of making the move and reestablishing himself.

At length, it was agreed that Salome, the three oldest daughters and the two boys would travel together. The two youngest girls would remain with their father and a housekeeper in Virginia and journey to Lancaster with him at a later date. It would be too difficult for Salome to handle very small children on a long trip by horseback, the only practical way the large family could travel.

Salome argued that the youngest should accompany her rather than stay with their father, but he insisted that she needed all the support she could get, support which could come only from the older, more dependable children. He pointed out that all sorts of calamities could befall small children on the trail, from accidents and illness, to becoming lost or stolen.

In the end, Salome agreed reluctantly to the plan and the little band set out. The further she traveled, the more apprehensive she grew about her husband. They had never been apart for long and she could not dismiss how distressed the fever had made him. Indeed, the more she thought about it, the more worried she became that he would never recover sufficiently to make the journey by himself, let alone with the two small children.

Salome's horse led the way. Behind were Thomas and his older sisters Betsy and Sofia sharing a mount, while Mathew and

Susan brought up the rear. They traveled northward along the Patapsco Road, not far from Maryland's Thomas Creek Valley where they had lived for four years before circumstances took them to Baltimore, then on to Alexandria, Virginia.

This return journey through the lush valley was somber, despite the glorious October weather. Already the trees were turning magnificent shades of red and gold. The air was fresh and sweet with the aroma of hay newly mown and of apples ripening in nearby orchards.

Under any other circumstances, their passage through Maryland's mellow countryside would have been a treat beyond description. Instead, it was funereal in tone. They were retreating from a happy, fulfilling life in Loudoun County, Virginia faced with the burden of surviving the oncoming winter without Thomas at the helm.

Salome noted frequently along the way how much busier the road was than she remembered it being when they traveled the route in happier times nearly a decade earlier. Now more travelers and settlers were moving readily from one state to another. As the young nation gathered strength in its independence, many men and their families were plunging into new ventures, some into business or trades which required frequent long-distance travel, others leaving their homes forever to seek a new life in settlements springing up to the west or in eastern towns growing to meet the economic demands of a new country.

Men passing the little family along the road recognized that Salome Atkinson was a gracious lady leading a well-mannered brood. They paused to tip their hats or bid the time of day no matter how surly or thoughtless they might have acted toward other fellow travelers.

By the next evening, the little group knew that York was not far. Traffic on the road was increasing, with more and more Conestoga wagons passing by in quest of an easy passage across the Alleghenies. At York, travelers heading west found several forks in the road to contemplate. Most pioneers took the Monacacy Road to Fort Cumberland and the booming Wills Creek settlement, but others selected the more northern route over the mountains by way of Fort Littleton and Fort Ligonier.

Salome and her children were headed in the opposite direction, east to Lancaster. Once past York, the settlements increased in number. Quaker and Presbyterian meeting houses dotted the road every ten miles. By the time they boarded Wright's Ferry for the ride across the Susquehanna River, Salome sensed that she was home. To her children, however, it was a strange new land. They had lived so many years in Virginia that their birthplace was but a dream, a dream supported by stories their parents had told them of life at an earlier time.

Upon arriving at their destination, they all moved in with Salome's aunt, Elizabeth Gitter Heffley, who made her home in the village of Ephrata. There they awaited word, hoping each day that Thomas and the two youngest children had set forth upon their way.

As time elapsed, Salome became uneasy. Her children often found her staring out of the window, awaiting the post, and nervously twisting her hands. When the letter finally came, Salome sat silently for a long time. The children studied her face, not daring to guess the awful news. At last, Salome spoke, "Children, I am afraid that your father is dead."

The fever had been too much for him. He died and was buried in a Virginia grave several weeks before his wife and children in Pennsylvania knew what had happened. The long-awaited letter had been written by a Virginia neighbor who promised to care for the two small children until spring.

At first, Salome Atkinson had no idea what to do. She was left with seven children to support and she despaired of being able to cope with the problem until young Thomas pointed our her great asset, an excellent education.

"Since you have taught us so well, why not teach others?"

Salome smiled for the first time in months. Her oldest son's suggestion was the perfect solution. Donning her bonnet and shawl, she rushed out the door. Within a few hours, she learned of an open teaching position in nearby Reamstown and was quickly accepted. That accomplished, her next step was to find proper situations for her oldest children.

Elizabeth and Sophia were lovely young ladies, willing

and able to help. Once their circumstances were understood, several relatives, all prominent members of the community, invited them to donate their time and effort to teaching and amusing the younger children in return for learning the fine arts of sewing, cooking, and performing on the spinet, accomplishments expected of genteel young ladies. In exchange for their services, Salome made certain that her stunning daughters were introduced to the eligible men of the area.

As soon as the first buds of green appeared on trees that had been dormant throughout the winter, young Thomas proposed that he and Mathew ride back to Virginia for the two young girls.

Sophia protested at first. "You're much too young to make such a journey by yourselves."

Thomas reassured her, convincing her that he remembered the way and would return with the girls, each one sharing a horse with their brothers.

Salome smiled, seeing a trace of her optimistic husband in

her son. She knew that the younger children would be no problem. She could keep them with her and instruct them along with her students.

Thomas and Mathew, however, needed professions. Since they no longer had a father to emulate, they must be placed with master craftsmen in order to learn a trade.

Thomas had no difficulty deciding what he would like to do. For years, he had cherished stories his mother told him about the great statesman, Benjamin Franklin. After learning to read, Thomas devoured <u>Poor Richard's Almanac</u> and everything else Franklin wrote. There was no question in his mind; he would become a printer, exactly like his idol, Benjamin Franklin.

Being younger and having no burning desire to pursue any profession in particular, Mathew decided that printing would do for him as well. Salome could not have been more pleased. With the help of friends, she located what she believed was an excellent situation for them as printing apprentices with Benjamin Mayer, the Ephrata community printer. There they would remain for seven years until they had mastered every aspect of the printing profession.

    Meanwhile, Elizabeth and Sophia were enjoying a social whirl. The most attractive young ladies for miles around, they quickly caught the attention of two respectable bachelors. By 1792, Elizabeth had married the accomplished Jacob Hibshman, who was destined to lead his state and nation as a judge, a Major General, an insurance company president, and a member of the U.S. House of Representatives, defeating James Buchanan for the seat. On June 2, 1794, Sophia married Joseph Gorgas, son of Jacob, the clockmaker and householder at the Ephrata community.

    As time passed, the widow Salome grew closer to her friends and relatives in Ephrata. She frequently visited the printing shop to learn how her sons were doing and soon became ensnared by the influence wielded by the Cloister that dominated the community of Ephrata and its residents. Relieved of the burden of marrying off her older daughters and pleased that her sons had secured their future, Salome retreated into the Cloister, leaving her younger daughters, Sarah, Penelope, and Susan, with her aunt.

The Brethren soon discovered that Salome, like her amorous parents, had no intention of abiding by the Cloister regulations. She was not the celibate type. Neither was Mayer. Lonely, uncommonly beautiful, and tempestuous by all accounts, Salome fell into a liaison with the printer, who was at least ten years her junior.

The affair threw the Cloister into a turmoil and prompted brother John Frederick to fling a full chamber pot through her open window. Salome and Mayer, their tryst exposed, ran after and attacked the retreating brother until they were apprehended and dragged before the justice of the peace on assault and battery charges.

The sordid affair sealed Salome's expulsion. A manuscript preserved at the Cloister State Historic Site reads: "At a Conference held…the 11th Day of February 1797 by the Elders and members of the German Religious Society called Seven-day Baptists at Ephrata…it appeared to said conference that Salome Atkinson, one of the Sisters of the said society, has for a length of time past created great disorder and Confusion in the said society and lives in open Violation of their Civil and religious principles…We the Elders and Members of the Said Society…do declare the said Salome Atkinson be henceforth Suspended and Debarred from all Rights and Privileges of the said Society Whatsoever."

Salome tossed her nose and skirts at the Cloister by marrying Mayer and moving to Harrisburg. There Mayer began publishing the <u>Harrisburger Morgenrithe</u> newspaper in 1799. Despite an intellectual bent suggested by the large and varied library detailed in his will, Mayer's character and personal devotion to Salome, then in her mid-forties, are suspect.

In a letter to Jacob Hibschman, he cites the melancholy death of Salome's grandchild in a kettle of boiling water and remarks, "…the old Woman has a mind to go to Virginia." He made no effort to send Salome to her grieving daughter, but he lost no time in remarrying on August 1, 1809 following Salome's death in March of the same year.

Perhaps Mayer's true character is best described by Mathew Atkinson in a letter he sent to Jacob Hibshman in August 1809. Besides lamenting his personal and financial woes, he says. "…as to old Mayer, I have but little regard or ever had, or ever shall have because his treatment to me has been base and malicious, and for all that ever he did for me, which was little or nothing, I thank him not…I wish him a heartfelt repentance of the many crimes which I believe him to have been guilty of, that he may go again to Ephrata and seclude himself in the brother house, a fit place for his repentance and amendment, a fit companion for the bats and midnight screech owl which no doubt infest that place."

Thomas, Jr., the only one of Salome's children to lead a fulfilling life, learned his printing lessons well before distancing himself from Mayer. After trundling a used Franklin press over the mountains to Meadville, Pennsylvania, he established The Crawford Messenger, the second newspaper published west of the Allegheny Mountains. A generous good citizen, he contributed to society in many ways, including serving as

Treasurer of Crawford County from 1820-1832, as representative to the Pennsylvania State Legislature from 1826-1836, and as a founder of Allegheny College.

Thomas Atkinson's siblings knew misfortune far better than happiness. Elizabeth Atkinson Hibshman died at 39 leaving six young children. Sarah Atkinson Albright lost three of her seven children before her own death in 1841. Her husband, a physician, became blind at an early age, adding greater burden to the family. Mathew Atkinson attempted one failed job after another and lost all but two of more than a dozen children. Penelope Atkinson Boyer either deserted or divorced her husband, living until old age with her only son in Harrisburg. Susan Atkinson Fremole may have left or lost her husband by 1830 when she is listed as head of household. Since no additional trace of her is found in official records, the place, date, and cause of her death are unknown.

Sophia Atkinson Gorgas and her husband prospered initially by operating a saw mill, a hotel, and a cotton processing mill, but after losing everything because of a friend's malicious interference, they moved frequently and raised ten children amid great hardship.

Their tenth and youngest son, Josiah Gorgas, had little formal education until his sister Elizabeth and her husband, Daniel Chapman, invited him to stay with them in Lyons, New York. After completing a local newspaper apprenticeship, he began reading law in the office of Graham Chapin. The New York congressman was so impressed by Josiah's ability and desire to learn that he nominated him for a West Point appointment. The young man was accepted.

Upon graduating sixth in his class in June 1841, Josiah was assigned as assistant ordnance officer at Watervliet Arsenal near Troy, New York. Within the next two decades, he rose in rank. During a tour near Mobile, Alabama, he acquired as his bride Amelia Ross, daughter of a former governor of the state. When the Civil War broke out, he made the fateful decision to side with many West Point classmates and become Chief of the Confederate Ordnance Bureau.

Because of this action, Josiah was immediately alienated

from his family who supported the Union cause. His decision led to hardships after the fall of the South more severe than he had endured as a child. But he prevailed, and in September 1878 he became President of the University of Alabama. Just as he believed the worst was over, a series of strokes ensued, and he died on May 15, 1883, unaware that his eldest son, Dr. William Crawford Gorgas, was destined to be appointed as surgeon general of the U.S. Army in 1914. William earned this honor by conquering yellow fever, the disease that felled his grandfather, Thomas Atkinson, more than a century earlier.

Ephrata Cloister, Lancaster County, Pennsylvania

The silhouettes below are the property of Michele Clifton, Atkinson-Gorgas descendant

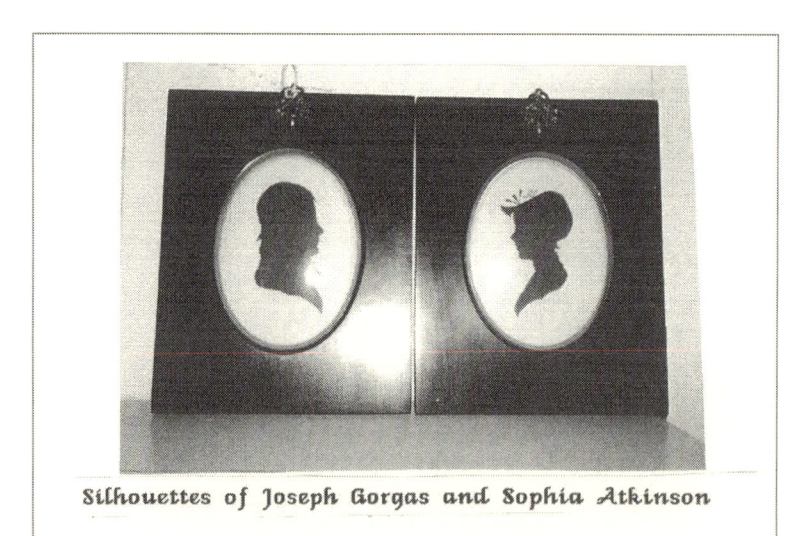

Silhouettes of Joseph Gorgas and Sophia Atkinson

REFERENCES

The Brethren Encyclopedia, Volume 1, A-J, Philadelphia, PA, 1983, pp. 448-452.

Chronicon Ephratense, pp. 215-216.

Egle's Notes and Queries, 4th series, vol. A, p. 133.

Egle's Notes and Queries of Pennsylvania, 1700-1800, Annual Volume 1806, XXX, pp. 168, 170.

Gorgas, Sophia Atkinson. Fragments of History of the Family of our Maternal Ancestor, Stephen Atkinson, by his granddaughter, Our Mother, dictated to and written by our brother Josiah Gorgas, 1840.

Lancaster County (Pennsylvania) Historical Society, Autumn 1962, pp. 167-175.

Leach, M.A. Papers. Genealogical Society of Pennsylvania.

McAllister, Anne Williams. Through Four Generations, self-published, 1996, pp. 21-30, 382-388.

Marquet, Cynthia. "Family Ties: The Atkinson-Mayer-Hibshman Story." Historical Society of the Cocalico Valley Newsletters, March-July 1997.

Montgomery, Berks County in the Revolution, p. 63.

Pennsylvania Archives, 2nd Series, Vol. XIV, p. 169.

Wiggins, Sarah Woolfolk, Editor. The Journals of Josiah Gorgas 1857-1878. The University of Alabama Press, 1995.

MARGARET FORSTER STEUART
1780-1835

The Belfast to Philadelphia sea lane across the Atlantic Ocean became the most popular route for Scotch-Irish immigrants sailing to the Pennsylvania colony during the 18th Century. Throngs of Ulster Scots sought the civil and religious liberties and kindly reception offered them in Pennsylvania where the Quaker influence with its profound love of all mankind was the cornerstone of society.

Outside of Philadelphia and the surrounding Welsh Tract, the first major settlements in the colony were in Chester County. The influx of colonists led to a division in 1729, the western portion becoming Lancaster County. When the burgeoning population warranted another split in 1785, the westernmost part of Lancaster County bordering the Susquehanna River became Dauphin County.

So it was that the Forster, Dickey, McFarland, and Bell families settled in Pennsylvania only once, yet lived and owned property in three different counties. It has not been determined if the families were acquainted in Northern Ireland, but they were like minded. Each sailed from Belfast early in the century, followed Indian trails into the wilderness, and ultimately claimed fertile acres in westernmost Paxton (also spelled Paxtang) Township a few miles east of the Susquehanna in the area destined to become Dauphin County. Paxton is today a suburb of Harrisburg.

Because most Scotch-Irish were Presbyterians, that denomination was dominant from Philadelphia to the Susquehanna. Meetinghouses were constructed at ten mile intervals along the main roadway in order that no family had to travel more than five miles to worship. Even before the early settlers completed construction on their own substantial log homes and barns, they rallied neighbors to erect the Paxton meetinghouse in 1716. Today it is recognized as the oldest Presbyterian church building in continuous use in Pennsylvania, and the second oldest in the United States.

By 1732, the original building had been enlarged to accommodate newcomers. It rapidly became the center of a thriving community noted for its outspoken pastor, Rev. John Elder, who received a rich theological education in Scotland before setting sail from Ulster. A proponent of freedom from government interference, he gained fame as Captain of the Paxton Rangers, all members of his congregation, and later as colonel of the Provincial government during the French and Indian Wars. From the beginning, Paxton families extended their camaraderie by topping off the Sunday services with a social gathering that included lunches on the lawn, weather permitting. Many generations of the founding families occupy the graveyard that sprang up adjacent to the meetinghouse.

About 1762, Catherine Dickey, daughter of celebrated

Indian fighter Moses Dickey, married John Forster, a farmer and active militia member, as were most men in the area. Their seventh and youngest child, Margaret, grew up in the closely knit community where girls knee-high to their mothers learned a multitude of adult tasks, from nurturing their younger siblings to preparing a hearty noon meal for the men toiling on the land. At day's end, when enormous pots had been scrubbed, the stone fireplaces and wooden floors swept clean, chickens beheaded and plucked, and the spinning wheel was still, they relaxed by candlelight perfecting a myriad of intricate stitches useful in making, repairing, and ornamenting garments and household linens.

Their male counterparts emulated their fathers and older brothers, helping to clear the land, raise crops, and tend the farm animals. Young boys were given guns as soon as they could lift them. They were on constant lookout for squirrels, rabbits, and larger game to put on the table, wolves preying on the flocks, and Indians from Conestoga Village who, upon one occasion, were the object of a raid by the Reverend John Elder's "Paxton Boys."

While Margaret was developing the household skills necessary for maintaining a family on the frontier, her brother, Thomas Forster, nearly twenty years her senior, received a good education as a surveyor. Like others his age, Thomas took up arms for the defense of the frontier during the Revolution. Once peace was achieved, he turned his attention to public service and was rewarded with responsible positions. A competent, masterful man, well liked by all who knew him, he was appointed as an associate judge of Dauphin County in 1793. During the whiskey insurrection of 1794, he served as colonel of a volunteer regiment in that expedition. His leadership earned him election to the Pennsylvania State Legislature as a representative, and in 1799 he was named the agent of the Harrisburg and Presque Isle Land Company, a position which took him to Erie and prominence as president of the Erie and Waterford Turnpike Company.

Margaret was only 17 years old when she and a neighbor, John McFarland, fell in love and were married in 1797. Their daughter born the following year was named Catherine, in keeping with the tradition of naming the first daughter after the maternal grandmother. Margaret had always been close to her older brother and John McFarland regarded him as a good friend, so when John Forster encouraged the young family to settle in the booming village of Erie, they gathered their belongings and made the move.

Their journey across the mountains took several weeks by wagon. As agreed in advance, they moved in with Forster, his wife Sarah, and their eight nieces and nephews until their own home was ready. By then, Margaret was expecting their second child, so the Forsters insisted that she remain with them until after the birth. Meanwhile, John McFarland began constructing a house with the help of other able men of the community. John Jr. was born on February 13, 1800. It should have been a joyous occasion, but the severe weather raging through the lakefront village felled McFarland, possibly with pneumonia. He died two weeks after the birth of his son, leaving his wife and children to rely on others for support.

John Forster immediately took his sister and her children

under his wing and provided for their care. Within a year, their sister Dorcas and her husband, William Bell, followed them from Paxton to Erie for the great opportunities promised by the lakeside location and businesses springing up. The Forster family, highly regarded by the townsfolk, was instrumental in introducing the Bells and Margaret to everyone of importance in the community. Among these was Thomas Steuart, a prosperous tailor and ensign in the militia Forster captained, the first company organized in the county.

    During social gatherings, Steuart became captivated by Margaret. Her cheerful personality, motherly attention to her children, and remarkable homemaking talents quickly drew him to the realization that marriage to her would add considerable joy to his bachelor life. He was 27 when Margaret, then 20, agreed to become his wife. Following the marriage performed on February 27, 1803 by Thomas Rees, the little family of four moved into Steuart's sturdy home, a two-storied log and frame building on Fourth Street facing the lake. Over the next nine years, two girls and five boys would arrive, adding to the couple's pride and

Margaret's boundless capacity to balance marriage, motherhood, and homemaking.

As the town grew in size, the Steuart family prospered. So did Margaret's brother, Thomas Forster, whose expertise and interest in many areas encompassed street commissioner and director and librarian of the town's first library company, along with his role as president of the Erie and Waterford Turnpike Company. Destined to serve as the Erie port collector under five presidents until his death, he provided community leadership throughout his life, but never at a more valuable time than in 1812 when relations between the United States and England soured and the new nation was thrown into another conflict.

The causes were threefold, primarily because of trade restrictions. Across the Atlantic Ocean, ongoing skirmishes between warships and privateers from both nations threatened shipping. The problem was further augmented by the posting of blockades along the seaboard by British ships.

Settlers inland did not escape the growing strife. They found themselves in the path of raids back and forth across the border with Canada, which was under English rule. The situation reached a head in January of 1813 when the U.S. Department of Navy ordered construction of ships at Erie under supervision of shipwright Noah Brown. Within two months, Major Commandant Oliver Hazard Perry arrived in Erie to take command of operations and plan for defense of Presque Isle.

    Because Erie was a young town, homes contained only the bare necessities. Throughout the spring and summer of 1813, the citizens were grateful for their meager belongings, all the easier to load into a wagon and flee inland fifteen miles to Waterford should the enemy arrive and occupy Erie. As one of the foremost matrons of the little village, Margaret Steuart was torn between caring for her family and doing her share for the community's war preparations. Army units were stationed nearby, while the lake harbor, barely two blocks from her home, was filled with U.S. Naval vessels in various stages of construction.

    Worries mounted and rumors abounded at every street corner and doorway. As each day dawned, Margaret wondered if the time had come to load her family's belongings onto a wagon and escape. An evacuation plan devised by her husband and other village leaders seemed to be the best hope of eluding certain British invasion, but Margaret and many citizens resolutely remained in Erie.

Perhaps Margaret stood firm because self-reliance was an integral part of her heritage. Every inch as stalwart as her ancestors, she had no intention of deserting her husband and other military men in Erie until the settlement was clearly doomed. So it was that she never budged, even when the battle between American and British ships raged on the water within sight and sound of her home.

The smoke from cannon fire was swirling across the harbor the day Margaret's brother, now Colonel Forster, stopped by to introduce Oliver Hazard Perry, a guest in his home, just around the corner on French Street.

Margaret listened to Perry's account of the battle that earlier had taken the life of Captain James Lawrence on the frigate USS "Chesapeake." Moved by the dying officer's last words, she asked Perry how the women of Erie could participate and prove their patriotism.

Perry had observed her needlework skills in evidence around the room and made a request that astounded her: Would she construct a flag to inspire the battle-weary American sailors? Simple in design, it would bear the brave Lawrence's final plea, *"Don't give up the ship!"*

Swiftly enlisting the aid of her sister Dorcas Bell and her Forster nieces, Margaret completed and delivered the flag within a few days. Perry guarded the secret closely, planning to unfurl it before his men, should their courage begin to falter.

That moment arrived during the heat of the Battle of Lake Erie on September 10, 1813 between six British and nine American warships. The American sailors watched the flag being hoisted on Perry's flagship, the USS Brig "Lawrence," one of the nine vessels constructed during the summer at nearby Presque Isle. They had no idea what was about to transpire.

Within minutes, their hope was renewed. But the wind was light, preventing the "Lawrence" from making speed.

Unable to maneuver and avoid the cannon fire, it was severely damaged and disabled. The sight of the captain surrendering to the British dismayed the American sailors. For their part, the British expected the American vessels to retreat.

Both sides were unaware that Perry already had left the "Lawrence" and was fearlessly carrying the treasured flag to the USS Brig "Niagara" in an open boat, assisted by only a few men. He had no intention of surrendering. The moment the flag was hoisted once again on the warship, the cheering American sailors gained new strength and courage and performed magnificently.

Because of their actions and his superior leadership, Perry overcame the British fleet. He accepted their surrender on board the "Lawrence" in honor of his fallen comrade. Just as Perry had anticipated and Margaret Steuart had hoped, her simple flag helped the Americans achieve an impossible victory despite the British Navy's overwhelming strength.

Today Margaret's "Don't Give Up The Ship" flag is preserved in a case in the library of the United States Naval Academy at Annapolis, Maryland. It is about nine feet square of close woven, coarse muslin or sheeting, dark blue in color, and rather frequently patched. The letters are of white muslin, thirteen inches wide. The dark blue of the background is now quite rusty, while the letters are yellowed with age.

    Margaret's gift to posterity was accomplished with the help of her sister, Dorcas Bell, wife of Captain William Bell, and the Bell daughters, Jane and Elizabeth, both engaged to military men, Jane to Samuel Hays, and Elizabeth to James Tewksbury, who was badly wounded during the Battle of Lake Erie.

    To honor the friendship of her brother with Perry, Margaret also invited Forster's daughters, Elizabeth Rachel, Mary Theodosia, and Catherine Ann. They were experts at domestic chores, having kept house for their father since the death four years earlier of their mother, the former Sarah Petit Montgomery. Like the Bell girls, the Forster cousins were enthusiastic participants in the project, for their hearts were with men in the thick of the fighting. After the war, Elizabeth married James F. Herron, an artillery officer of the United States Army taken prisoner by the British. Mary Theodosia married Colonel

John Harris of the United States Navy, who became commandant of the Marine Corps, while Catherine Ann became the wife of Richard T. Timberlake, an officer of the fleet.

The Forster girls arrived with their little sisters, Hannah, eight, and Margaret, six. No matter that the youngest girls did little more than run errands, that moment in history remained fresh in their minds, and when it was time to choose a life partner, both married career Army men destined to become generals.

Hannah married Edward Vose Sumner, who led the cavalry charge at Cerro Gordo in the Mexican War and became Governor of New Mexico in 1851. Promoted to General during the Civil War, he was commander of the First Corps Army of the Potomac, was wounded at Antietam, and commanded one of General Burnside's three grand divisions at Fredericksburg.

Margaret married George Wright. As was the custom, she accompanied her husband wherever his command took him. Thus, en route to a new assignment shortly after the close of the Civil War, she and General Wright died together when the ship

"Brother Jonathan" sank off Portland, Oregon on July 30, 1865.

But when the young women gathered to create the flag destined to turn the tide of war, none envisioned what the future held. They knew only of the past, a heritage that prepared them for their role in that place and time.

By 1814, the Steuart family had moved to Meadville, another thriving western Pennsylvania town a short distance south of Erie in Crawford County. Thomas was drawn there by the community's need for a master weaver and the progressive local school where their children would study under scholars educated at major Eastern universities. As in Erie, both became productive and popular citizens. Margaret was only 55 when she died on January 16, 1835. The grieving Thomas then moved in with his stepson, John McFarland, and lived another three years, dying March 6, 1838 at age 62. Both were buried side by side at Mill Creek, Erie County.

If Margaret Forster Steuart could visit Erie today, she would find the Fourth Street site of her modest home occupied by Lafayette Place, an office complex. A few blocks away, at the foot of State Street near the public dock, the rotting hulk of Perry's flagship "Niagara" was transformed over a period of several years by 20th century artisans into the majestic tall ship that emerged victorious from the Battle of Lake Erie.

On September 10, 1988, the "Niagara," now the official flagship of the Commonwealth of Pennsylvania, slipped into the waters of Lake Erie. A cool breeze hovered about the shoulders of the onlookers. Some might have attributed it to autumn winds ruffling the chilly waters; others were not beyond believing that it was the spirit of Margaret Forster Steuart who never gave up the ship.

The following sketch of Margaret Forster Steuart from Egle's Notes and Queries, 1897, p. 159

Margaret Forster Steuart.

REFERENCES

Bell, Raymond Martin. <u>The Forster families of Paxton (now Dauphin County) Pennsylvania</u>, Washington, Pa, 1993, 22 pp.

Bell, Raymond Martin. <u>Three-Generation Genealogy of John Forster of Paxton</u>, Compiled April 15, 1992, 2 pp.

Commonwealth of Pennsylvania: Department of Public Instruction, State Library, Harrisburg. Letter from Albert Decker Keator, Director, State Library to Mrs. Lovett Frescoln, 500 Harvard Avenue, Swarthmore, Pa., June 10, 1947.

DAR Lineage Book #21, p. 17, National Number 20045.

DAR Lineage Book #27, p. 62, National Number 26172.

Dunaway, Wayland F. <u>The Scotch-Irish of Colonial Pennsylvania</u>, 1944.

Egle's <u>Notes and Queries of Pennsylvania</u>, Annual Volume 1897, pp. 157-160.

Egle's Notes and Queries of Pennsylvania, Series 1, Vol. 12, p. 250.

Egle's Notes and Queries of Pennsylvania, 170s-1800s, Series 1 and 2, Vol. 1, pp. 326-327.

Egle's Notes and Queries of Pennsylvania, 1700s-1800s, Series 1 and 2, Vol. II, p. 450.

Egle's Notes and Queries of Pennsylvania, Reprint Series 3, Vol. 1, p. 493.

Egle's Notes and Queries of Pennsylvania, 1700-1800s. Series 3, Volume II, pp. 402-403.

Egle's Notes and Queries of Pennsylvania, Series Three, Part 3, Vol. 5, p. 489.

Higgins, Betts, USNA Guide, Letter to Emily Pritchard Cary, July 15, 1980.

History of Erie County: Early Settlers of Erie County, Pennsylvania, 1884, p. 315.

Kelker, Luther Reilly. Forster Family - History of Dauphin County, Pa., with Genealogical Memoirs, Vol. III, pp. 559, 673-674.

Letters of Administration, Lancaster County, Pa.1749.

McAlarney, Mathias Wilson. Paxtang Sesqui-Centennial, 1890, p. 67.

Pennsylvania Archives, Warrants for Land, Series 3, Vol. 24, p. 70.

Pennsylvania Genealogies: Family of Forster, pp. 246-248.

Sanderson. Alfred. Perry's Flag. Egle's Notes and Queries, 1897, p. 160."…the old house with its memories, associations, joy and sorrows, heartaches and rejoicing, has disappeared in the march of time. The *Lawrence* has perished, lifted from the waters to be lost in fire; its patched and faded flag remains a memento to the American people of a great event in their history…and its story will have come to little purpose if…the women of our land permit the memory of its makers to become thin air."
Stewart Clan Magazine, Volume XIX, No. 6, 1941.

Wallace, Helen Bruce. Historic Paxton Her Days and Her Ways, 1722-1913, 1913. P. 14.

ROSE O'NEAL GREENBOW
1814-1864

Rose O'Neal Greenhow was born Maria Rosetta O'Neal on a plantation in Port Tobacco, Montgomery County, Maryland, a location that is today part of Charles County. She was the third child of John O'Neale and Eliza Henrietta Hamilton whose marriage on January 10, 1810 was registered in Prince George's County, Maryland. Two more children, a girl and a boy, followed Rose. The ancestors of both parents were Catholic arrivals during the 1600's seeking religious freedom. They received land grants from Lord Calvert who facilitated their emigration. By the early 1800s, their descendants had accumulated considerable more property and social stature.

Rose's earliest known ancestor was Conn O'Neill, known as Bacach the Lame, the first Earl of Tyrone, Northern Ireland. Conn's son, "Shane the Proud," was usurped and beheaded in Ireland in the early 1600s. Determined to protect Shane's son, James, Catholic priests sent him to Spain where he was raised at Court by the King of Spain. At the same time, the spelling of his surname was changed to Neale to hide his identity.

James Neale grew to adulthood and became a Captain of His Majesties Fleet. Upon his first glimpse of America in 1652, he was so impressed that he petitioned Lord Calvert for a land grant in the new world. Wollaston Manor, the plantation awarded him for services to the Crown, was constructed where the Potomac River meets its tributary, Wicomico River. It survived as a historical site until fire destroyed it in the early 20th Century. The descendants of James Neale were among the prominent Catholics of Maryland and married into the equally important Calvert, Bealle, Van Swearingen, Digge, and Wathen families

Rose's grandfather, Lawrence O'Neale, was not only an early land speculator in western Montgomery County, but he also served numerous terms as a member of Maryland's House of Representatives. When his son, John, married into the wealthy Hamilton family of Prince George's County, it marked the merger of two major Maryland landowners.

John and Eliza might have moved initially into Wollaston Manor and the published accounts stating that Rosa was born there could be correct. However, their descendant, John W. O'Neal II, recently conducted considerable research of primary sources and learned that John had a home for his family built in western Montgomery County between the towns of Poolesville and Barnesville. There he soon settled into the life of a gentleman planter. Family records dating back to 1816 found at St. Mary's Catholic Church in Barnesville suggest that Rose and her siblings spent most of their childhood at the new home, rather than at Port Tobacco.

John W. O'Neal's research also shatters other accounts claiming that Rosa's mother died first and Rosa became an orphan at the death of her father. In fact, Rosa's father was the cause of the family misfortunes. Indeed, one wonders how John O'Neale had time to manage his extensive plantation between indulging frequently in such popular sports as dog races, cockfights, and womanizing. His death was a direct result of too much drink. The popular explanation appeared in a book by Ishbel Ross published in 1954. O'Neal discovered a more logical ending.

    According to Ross, John O'Neale and his Negro servant, Jacob, were returning from a night of drinking and were nearly home when Jacob knocked O'Neale off his horse. To get rid of his master once and for all, Jacob killed him with a blow on the head.

    O'Neal presents another explanation, one that implicates family members for plotting the death of a relative who embarrassed those with political positions and aspirations by his gambling and pursuit of unseemly women. At the very least, once their black sheep was dead, they contrived a way to avoid blame by pinning it on Jacob. At that period in history, northern

"Black Politicians" were promoting the freeing of slaves. Inspired by their rhetoric and lacking witnesses, it was easy for those responsible for the crime to accuse Jacob. By taking refuge in the slavery issue, the family saved face and hid the seamy side of O'Neale's life from the public.

Historical records O'Neal found at the Maryland State Archives in Annapolis contain witness statements and evidence that John had spent a day drinking at Nathan Trail's Tavern and kindly shared more than a glass of whiskey with his servant. The two started home together on the proverbial dark and stormy night. When John's horse was unable to travel fast on the wet ground, he told Jacob to go on ahead.

Jacob awoke the next morning still drunk. Unable to find his master at home, he set out looking for him. Not far from the house, he came upon O'Neale bleeding and unconscious. Was he the victim of an attack or an accident? Afraid that blame for the injury would be placed on him, Jacob picked up a rock and smashed John's skull. The doctors who testified at the hearing could not decide if John died from the initial fall or from a blow on the head. The upshot was that Jacob was tried, convicted, and sentenced. He was hung in the Rockville, Maryland public square on Friday, October 10, 1817.

John O'Neale's estate, though large, did not begin to cover his gambling obligations. For the next few years, Rose's mother fought creditors and refused to sell their home, known as "Conclusion." The aptness of the name was realized when Eliza eventually agreed to the sale. Many writers have indicated that Rose and her siblings were shuffled about between relatives while their mother was trying to administer her husband's estate, but O'Neal has found no accounts confirming that they lived anywhere other than at the family home during this period.

He is confident that Rose and her siblings were educated at St. Mary's Church in Barnesville and by their mother and their widowed Aunt Eleanor, as well. By the time Rose's life changed dramatically, she had read many great books and histories responsible for her strong opinions about the social and economic impact of wars. These, along with her distrust of the northern "Black Politicians" became the basis of her philosophy.

John O'Neale's wasteful ways finally caught up with his widow. Forced to sell "Conclusion" to settle his lingering debts, she sent her daughters Rose and Eleanor to live with their Aunt Mary Hill. At first glance, the move to a veritable boarding house could have seemed demeaning to young girls used to living in a plantation manor house, but the Capitol Hotel, located at 1st and A Streets in Washington, DC, was a magnificent structure. It was built originally to house Congress temporarily after the British burned down the capitol during the War of 1812. Situated in the social center of the city, it offered Rose amenities and valuable contacts that would influence the rest of her life.

Aunt Mary Hill operated Capitol Hotel as a home away from home for many distinguished senators and statesmen. Evenings spent around the dining table often firmed decisions made the very next day at the White House and in Congress. Rose listened raptly to the discussions taking place among the guests and became so enamored of the political process that she began visiting the Senate regularly. After sitting through the daily debates, she paid strict attention to the conversations in the

Hotel Lounge where the influential men retired after consuming the hearty evening meal to plan the next day's strategy.

    Rose soon mastered the art of debate so well that she discussed politics with those men of importance at every opportunity. The acquaintances she cultivated at the hotel and on the staffs of the daily newspapers kept her up to date on everything happening in the hallowed government halls. In her mind, she worked over the accumulated information for debate ammunition. Before long, she was expressing her opinions to the likes of John C. Calhoun, James Buchanan, Andrew Jackson, and James Madison, all fellow residents of Capitol Hotel at various times. They returned the admiration she felt for them by treating her with the kind of deference they afforded their peers. When she was not attending sessions of Congress, she listened to Chief Justice John Marshall in the Supreme Court.

    Rose's friendship with James Madison and his wife Dolley led to a union of their families. Eleanor, Rose's sister, was introduced to and later married Dolley's nephew, James Madison Cutts. That family connection provided ample opportunity for Rose to cultivate Dolley's friendship so intimately that Dolley invited Robert Greenhow, a prominent lawyer and author, to the boardinghouse to meet her young friend.

Greenhow was the son of John Greenhow, the Mayor of Richmond, Virginia, whose wife perished in a theater fire when their son was 12 years old. Even though he was twice her age by the time they met, Robert was instantly attracted to Rose. They were married in 1835. At 43, Robert was well established both socially and career-wise. A translator, writer, and interpreter for the State Department, he had graduated from William and Mary College before doing graduate work at Columbia University and later studying law at the Sorbonne in Paris. Although one source says that Rose was 26 at the time of her marriage, it is more likely that she was 21 based on documents stating that she was 23 in 1837. Already married, she appeared that year at the Montgomery County, Maryland Courthouse in company with her sisters for the filing of court records to settle the family estate after the death of their mother.

By then, Rose and Robert had welcomed their first child, Florence, born in 1836. Gertrude arrived in 1838, the year after the court records were filed, and Leila in 1840. Their next four children born in 1842, 1845, 1848, and 1849 died at an early age. Their last child, "Little Rose," born April 2, 1853, would play a key role in her mother's future.

Throughout their marriage, Rose assisted Robert in his written projects and served as the perfect hostess at their lavish parties. Their home in Washington was a four-story Georgian-style mansion directly across Lafayette Park from the White House. It was staffed with servants who handled all the chores, allowing her ample time for socializing and analyzing the latest news about the growing threat of abolition. Robert's close friend, John C. Calhoun, frequently visited and encouraged Rose's sympathy for the Southern viewpoint.

Steeped in Rose's example, her daughters Florence, Gertrude and Leila grew up to be opinionated and independent young ladies. When Florence announced plans to marry Treadwell Moore, a Northern Army Officer, Rose may have been shocked and disappointed, but she understood the need to follow one's heart.

Whenever the opportunity arose, Rose traveled around the country with Robert, even to Mexico on several occasions. Early in 1853, Rose, Gertrude, and Leila accompanied Robert on a business trip to San Francisco. Rose was pregnant with their youngest daughter, so when the time drew near for the birth, she and the two older girls returned to Washington in February while Robert remained to complete his work.

Robert may have returned home for a brief stay during the year, but he was working in San Francisco early the following year when he slipped off one of the city's plank sidewalks and toppled down a steep embankment to the street below. He did not let Rose know about the severe injury to his leg because he did not think it was serious enough for her to rush to his side in San Francisco. She had no idea of his condition and was not informed when the injured leg became paralyzed. His death in March 1854 is chronicled in an obituary in the *Daily Alta California*.

Upon learning of Robert's death, Rose immediately

traveled to San Francisco, leaving Little Rose in the care of her sister. She successfully sued the city and was awarded $10,000, a large sum of money at that time. No doubt she also received a healthy amount from Robert's estate. In any event, she continued to live well in Washington as a widow, purchasing a fine house at 398 16th Street opposite St. John's Episcopal Church. Still beautiful, personable, and active socially, she remained in black after the period of mourning elapsed. Nevertheless, the severity of her attire did not deter her from living a life of excitement and intrigue. Indeed, it served to thrust her into the limelight just as it enabled her to avoid suspicion of pursuing illicit romance or other evils.

  The case in point was a possible romantic relationship with Senator Henry Wilson who would be elected Vice-President after the Civil War to President Ulysses Grant. Rose's alleged friendship with the Republican from Massachusetts was curious. He not only was married, but he also opposed slavery. No matter, love letters found in her possession were attributed to him. Although no direct proof of a love affair has ever been confirmed, many accounts exist of their warm friendship and frequent meetings. Was their relationship based on passion or merely her dogged determination to coax every morsel of information possible from an acquaintance in great power?

Rose wasted no time expressing her opinion, wherever she went, that the federal government had no right to force southern states to abolish slavery. John C. Calhoun, her idol, was responsible for stoking that belief within her. During his final illness in 1850, she was his constant companion. After his death, his views became even more important to her. She firmly believed that the Northern politicians she regarded as "Black Republicans" were violating the constitution when they diminished the powers of state governments. Adamant to a fault, she supported slavery as it was practiced in the South. She was certain that Southern economy could not prosper without it and vowed to do everything within her power to help thwart Abolition.

Rose went out of her way to cultivate friendships with important men. William H. Seward, Col. Erasmus D. Keyes, and

Senator Joseph Lane of Oregon were favorites in her stable of movers and shakers. She was so close to James Buchanan of Pennsylvania that she journeyed to California to support his candidacy for President. After he was elected, they were often seen walking together. Throughout his term, she continued to entertain friends from both the North and South, but her heart remained with the South.

Having been raised on property encompassing extensive acreage cultivated by slaves, she was constantly reminded of her privileged status by the family lifestyle. The sight of slaves toiling over the fields did not conflict with her love of nature. In recalling her childhood, she remembered skipping happily through the garden, often in the company of children her own age whose parents were household slaves. No matter that she shared youthful pleasures with them, her own feelings of superiority cemented her approval of the slavery system that allowed the privileged minority to utilize the services of the downtrodden for personal benefit. For so long as she lived, her convictions never wavered. Unwilling to shift her stand, she choreographed her own destruction.

John O'Neal, her descendant, believes that Rose's greatest flaw, the one that drove her to self-destruction, was her love of money. She was born into a world where slavery was a way of life necessary for those who benefited from it. For generations, her family had owned slaves, as did every family of importance in the South. It would not be surprising to learn that Rose was regarded by those beneath her social level as a snob, a woman who worshiped education and influential connection above compassion for her fellow man. A confessed student of the U.S. Constitution, she was convinced that the "Black Republicans" were flirting with treason and she vowed to prevent them from destroying the society to which she was accustomed. It was clear to her that most of the slaves, once they became free, would head north for employment opportunities that paid salaries. Without extensive labor resources, the Southern economy would collapse. Consequently, she despised those who were dead set on destroying the only way of life that would enable her to maintain her gentility.

To call her conceited would not be an exaggeration. After moving to Washington as a teenager, she cultivated a taste for the finer things of life. Her aunt moved in the most elite social circles and made certain that her young charge was introduced to people who mattered. Upon meeting her, they eagerly included her in their cliques. As Rose grew into young womanhood, her stunning features caused men to stop in their tracks whenever she passed. Soaring socially, she attracted many beaus, each boasting an impeccable social reputation and substantial fortune that could easily provide for a family and a wife with expensive tastes. With Dolley Madison's help, she had found the perfect husband, one who answered all her needs and desires.

Widowhood might have been a blow to a less ambitious woman. Although it altered her situation to some degree, she had not forgotten how to use her assets to her advantage. Still beautiful, opinionated, and adept at devious methods guaranteed to capture hearts and lower suspicion, she employed her wiles and used flattery to coax information from northern officers stationed in Washington. As the winds of war grew, Rose endured another tragedy, the death of her daughter Leila in 1860. Still, she did not waver in her plot to prevent the North from achieving its goals.

Wealthy Southern planters and socialites became somber when Abraham Lincoln was elected President on November 6, 1860. South Carolina seceded from the Union on December 20, 1860. Four more states followed within two months, and Jefferson Davis became president of the Confederate States of America. Rose scarcely paused to mourn the death of her daughter Gertrude in March of 1861. Her destiny demanded strict attention.

Using her social connections and popularity, Rose made certain that her considerable opinions were expressed to the right people. It did not take long for her sympathies to reach Col. Thomas Jordan. An officer in the U.S. Army, he had not yet resigned and joined the Confederacy when he approached Rose about developing a Confederate spy ring. She leaped to the challenge and by April 1861, she not only had mastered the cipher code he shared, but also had developed a network of spies.

Some came from ordinary circumstances; others were sympathetic government officials and prominent citizens residing in or near Washington. Jordan, now using the alias Thomas J. Rayford, continued to plot with Rose right through his conversion to the Confederate Army in May 1861 when he joined General Beauregard's staff.

Although Rose may have instigated less publicized coups, her reputation grew from the First Battle of Manassas. Soon after the war began, the Northern public believed that it could be won quickly and easily. The Union military leaders concurred. Their objective was to march to Richmond, the Confederate capitol, and cut off supplies, thereby ending the strife. Rose's goal was to sabotage their plan. Upon learning from her contacts that Union General Irvin McDowell planned to advance from Washington southward on July 16th, she made her move.

Her scheme was to alert General P.G.T. Beauregard, encamped near Bull Run, that McDowell's army was about to go on the move. It would march through Arlington, Alexandria,

Fairfax, and Centreville en route to Manassas Junction where they would demolish the railroad tracks. She launched her ingenious plot by recruiting Betty Duvall, one of many willing servants she called her "little birds." Young, pretty, and dressed in the typical attire of a farm girl to avoid arousing suspicion, Betty made her way to Chain Bridge. Once she crossed over the Potomac River to the Virginia side, she changed into riding attire, mounted a horse, and rode like the wind to Fairfax Courthouse where General Milledge L. Bonham was stationed.

Upon informing Bonham that she had an important message for General Beauregard, Betty proceeded to remove the comb from her hair and produce the ciphered note hidden in her thick locks. Bonham is quoted as saying, "She let fall the longest and most beautiful roll of hair I have ever seen. She then took from the back of her head, where it had been safely tied, a small package, not larger than a silver dollar, sewed up in silk."

Bonham received the message from Betty Duvall on July 10th allowing time to relay it to Beauregard. By the time the Union army neared Centreville, the Confederate troops awaited them. Initially, defeat of Beauregard's small, untested Confederate army seemed certain. But prospects changed two days later when General Joseph E. Johnston and his Confederate reinforcements arrived unexpectedly from the Shenandoah Valley. Instead of the decisive win they envisioned, the Union troops were trounced by the Southern forces. Many gave up and began running back toward Washington.

Overjoyed that her role was instrumental in Beauregard's victory, Rose wasted no time tooting her own horn. Her descendant John O'Neal believes that she deliberately sought to be recognized and feted as a Southern woman who managed to outwit the Northern army through feminine wiles. Certainly the word traveled rapidly to President Jefferson Davis who sent her a letter praising her for efforts that sealed the win at Bull Run.

Rose's hand in the Northern army's debacle was even acknowledged by President Lincoln, who remarked that she knew more about what went on in his cabinet meetings than he himself knew. Even if Rose was not responsible for seeding the rumors, the local newspapers propelled her into the open with articles applauding her remarkable accomplishment as a Confederate spy...and a woman, at that.

Unlike most spies, Rose appeared to thrive as word spread about her role in embarrassing the North. She sloughed off suggestions of impropriety even as her home became a center of intrigue. Generals, senators, diplomats and young officers visited her house at all hours of day and night. Little time passed before Allan Pinkerton became privy to her antics.

The Scottish immigrant's knack for detective work had catapulted him into a position as head of the Union Secret Service guarding President Lincoln. He accused Rose of being a traitor and manipulating the behavior of Army officers through her feminine wiles. Instead of curtailing her trysts to cool his investigations, she remained defiant and continued operating her band of spies right under his nose.

Pinkerton was no fool. After spying on Rose and Senator Henry Wilson through an open window one night, he arrested Rose on August 23, 1861. For several months, she was held under house arrest in her own home with her daughter Little

Rose. Defying Pinkerton, Rose used her secret contacts to send a letter to William H. Seward, President Lincoln's Secretary of State. A copy made its way to the *Richmond Whig*, which published it in full. Was it conveyed through one of Rose's associates, or did Seward himself pass it along to the editor as a favor to his lady friend? In either case, it reached the public, causing a stir in both North and South. Excerpts from her letter follow:

"Sir, For nearly three months I have been confined, a close prisoner, shut out from air and exercise, and denied all communication with family and friends…On Friday, August 23, without warrant or other show of authority, I was arrested by the Detective Police, and my house taken in charge by them; that all my private letters, and my papers of a life time, were read and examined by them; that every law of decency was violated in the search of my house and person, and the surveillance over me… (D)uring the first days of my imprisonment, whatever *necessity* forced me to seek my chamber, a detective stood sentinel at the open door and I, with my little child, was placed absolutely at the mercy of men without character or responsibility…

"I am yet ignorant of the causes of my arrest; that my house has been seized and converted into a prison by the Government; that the valuable furniture it contained has been abused and destroyed; that during some periods of my imprisonment I have suffered greatly for want of proper and sufficient food."

Rose fully intended to shock the public by listing the indignities she suffered and describing how soldiers watched her and sniggered with amusement as she attended to private matters. She was further insulted by the arrival of other female prisoners to her home, women whom she regarded as "of the lowest class." Her once beautiful home became known as Fort Greenhow. Still, nothing Pinkerton or his staff did could stifle her regular communications with the South.

On the pretense of a passion for needlework, she requested that skeins of yarn be brought to her. The arriving packages were carefully inspected by the soldiers stationed at her door; they did not realize that Rose was able to skillfully conceal codes within the finished handiwork passed along to her spies. As it became clear to authorities that Rose was using conspirators to spread secret messages, the decision was made to commit her to a more confined place.

Her destiny was the Old Capital Prison. Ironically, this was the very same building that served as the Capitol Hotel, the lively boarding house once owned by her Aunt Mary Hall, the very place where she acquired her taste for politics and politicians. She and Little Rose, then eight years old, were lodged in the room where she had visited her hero, Senator Calhoun, during his last days.

She wasted no time continuing her literary assault on Northern "cruelty" and conveying it by surreptitious means to the Southern press. Her communications stressed the squalid conditions under which she and her young daughter were forced to live. Little Rose even came down with measles during the ordeal. In the eyes of readers, she became a martyr for the Southern cause.

Rose was defiant at her May 1862 hearing on charges of

espionage. She hinted that her informers were double agents, followers of Lincoln's government, yet prepared to put their own lives in peril by passing along secrets to bring it down. She recalled the ordeal at that trial in her diary of March 25, 1863, later published in London as *"Diary of a Confederate Spy."*

Upon receiving her summons to appear before United States commissioners for the trial of state prisoners, she obeyed and was taken to the provost marshal who occupied the house of a Mrs. Gwin, once the site of happy, hospitable gatherings. She wrote:

"I passed up through the filthy halls and stairs, was conducted to the third story, and put in a room without fire, and kept there until my hands and feet were completely benumbed with cold. A guard…stationed at the door…rattled his musket in order that I should have a comfortable sense of his proximity. Numbers of officers in gay uniforms came in, upon one pretext or another, in order to stare at me."

When informed that she was charged with treason, she replied that she had studied the Constitution of the United States and found no provision to justify the charge. After a lengthy exchange of opinions, she emphasized that her daughter was exposed to treatment that could seriously impair her health. The trial ended with the commissioners deciding to exile her to Richmond into the care of the Confederate states headed by President Jefferson Davis. She was returned to prison to await further action.

The first step toward her release came in mid-May 1862, when Henry Wilson visited her room. There is no record of what transpired, but he may have wanted to let her know that he was doing everything he could to hasten her release. Shortly after he called on Rose, she, Little Rose, and several female prisoners were taken to Baltimore by train. There they were placed on a boat that sailed to Fort Monroe, Virginia, also known as Freedom Fortress. The only stone fort encircled by a moat, it was located off Hampton and remained in Union hands throughout the war. On July 2, 1862, after pledging not to return north of the Potomac River during the hostilities, Rose and her companions were transferred to a train and taken to Richmond.

There, accompanied by Little Rose, she was welcomed as a heroine and rewarded by President Davis for her efforts. She thoroughly enjoyed her stay in that city, but had barely enough time to relish her freedom before President Davis proposed an exciting way for her to promote the Confederate cause overseas. To carry out his wishes, she would sail to Britain and undertake a tour of that country and of France.

The first leg of her journey took her to Charleston, South Carolina, presumably to board a ship that would take her across the Atlantic Ocean. She arrived in the city on July 15, 1863, just as its residents were becoming concerned about its fall. Along the way she had met with General Robert E. Lee and conveyed her impression of his confidence in a letter to President Davis dated July 16, 1863. During their meeting, she informed Lee about the city's "imminent peril," the booming of heavy guns and mortars, and the general panic displayed by both citizens and military.

In a letter dated July 20, 1863, she described to Alexander Boteler, a member of the Confederate States House of

Representatives, the "fearfully grand" naval and land attack on Charleston resulting in the defeat of the Union forces. Ever mindful of those severe conditions, she digressed about the "delightful weather," the mosquitoes bothering her daughter, and wished "with all my heart" that Boteler was with her in Charleston.

Was he one of her many paramours who furthered her plots, or merely a friend in conspiracy? It is interesting that letters to him continued until her romantic fortunes changed.

She closed that letter with the information that she was about to go to Wilmington, North Carolina. No doubt this was a necessary switch of plans. Perhaps her sources advised her that a sailing ship would find it easier to run the blockade from there rather than from Charleston.

To explain her departure from Charleston to casual friends in that city, she made certain that they were aware of her wish to rescue Little Rose from the terrors of war. She even hinted that, should the opportunity arise, she would send her daughter to a French convent. Thus, nobody was alarmed when both mother and daughter slipped away. Friends presumed that they had found a means of escaping the city and were already on the high seas.

The flight from Wilmington was more eventful than Rose had anticipated. The ship was challenged by Yankee cruisers throughout much of its run to St. George, Bermuda. Once she was safely settled there, she sent another letter to Boteler dated August 13, 1863. She reported that she had been seasick en route, but was recuperating and enjoying the climate, tropical flora, and friendship of the Reverend and Mrs. Walker, local Confederate sympathizers. Her plan, she confirmed, was to leave for Southampton the following week.

When Rose arrived in London with Little Rose, her daughter, Florence Moore, was already there. Because Florence's husband was a Union Army officer, her travel to London for the prearranged meeting had been easy to facilitate. It is not known if Florence was aware of her mother's true reason for being in London, but she was happy to help by enrolling Little Rose at the Sacred Hearts Convent in Paris.

With her little daughter in safe hands, Rose could operate to her best advantage. Now she was free to work around the clock influencing all British politicians and important people to sympathize with the Confederacy. Her true mission was underway.

It was December before Rose again wrote to Boteler, this time from her luxurious rooms at 3 Halkin Street, Grosvenor Place, London within two blocks of Buckingham Palace. Concerned that she had not heard from him, she feared that her letters had been intercepted. She expressed dismay at reading word in the Yankee press of the defeat at Lookout Mountain and conveyed her disappointment in the lack of mail from friends and associates back home.

Rose's disappointment at the dearth of letters from the South was more than balanced by her warm reception in London and her presentation at the court of Queen Victoria. Her stay in France was equally gratifying. There she was feted royally by the ruling classes, received at the court of Napoleon III, and granted an audience with the Emperor at the Tuileries. Upon returning to

London in mid-February, she took up residence at 157 New Bond Street in a genteel neighborhood around the corner from Piccadilly.

In a letter to Boteler dated February 17, 1864, she described her audience with the Emperor, who "treated me with great distinction, great kindness, and my audience in Court Circles was pronounced *"une grande success."* However, she warned that, "altho (sic) the Emperor was lavish of expressions of admiration of our President and cause, there was nothing upon which to hang the least hope of aid unless England acted simultaneously." She went on to observe, "…the French people are brutal ignorant and depraved to a degree beyond description and have no appreciation of our struggle which they believe is to free the slaves, and all their sympathies are really on the Yankee side."

Rose closed the letter with an account of her visits with British historian Thomas Carlyle and Cardinal Weisman and her plans to visit the House of Parliament. Except for the French public that she regarded as ignorant and inclined to favor the

North, she basked in sympathy for the South wherever she went. She even had time for romance, something she craved and had missed for many months.

This diversion came about through the friendship of Lady Georgiana Fullerton. Upon learning that Lady Fullerton's brother, the Second Earl Granville, was a widower, Rose quite likely employed her social skills to receive an introduction to the eligible gentleman. Granville, a liberal leader in the House of Lords who had lost his wife in 1860, was easily beguiled by the charming American heroine.

Following a brief period of courtship, the two became engaged. Although Rose made a strong case for the preservation of the Southern way of life during her stay in Great Britain, Granville remained neutral. His influence prevailed among the British cabinet, allowing the country's relations with the North to remain stable throughout the Civil War.

Once she became a permanent fixture on the arm of Granville, Rose was accepted wherever she traveled in England. When her book, "My Imprisonment and the First Year of

Abolition Rule at Washington," was published, it became an immediate bestseller. The royalties came rolling in, gold coin after gold coin. She set aside $2,000 as her personal gift to the Confederate treasury. Her own literary success was sealed, yet she rued the fact that the initial goal of her venture was to obtain British and French support for the Confederacy. In that, she had failed.

Admired by the British public and her distinguished gentleman friend, Rose must have believed that a brilliant future awaited her and her beloved Little Rose. But first she felt obliged to return to the Confederate States. In her possession were secret dispatches from the overseas spy network for key officers and government officials, as well as the royalties she intended to plow directly into the Confederate treasury. In the ship's hold were crates of lovely clothes for the Confederate women whose own smart gowns were worn.

Arrangements were made for her to sail on the *Condor,* a British blockade runner. The ship departed from Southampton in late September and first put in at Halifax, Nova Scotia. Their journey southward encountered no problems until nearly home. Then, on the evening of Friday, September 30, 1864, the ship was off the coast near Wilmington, North Carolina when it was observed by a Union gunboat. The captain, hoping to avert a battle, raced towards shore ahead of the gunboat. But a severe storm was brewing and he ran aground at about midnight on what is described in many accounts as a sandbar at the mouth of the Cape Fear River. In his book, William Gilmore Beymer identifies the object as the wreck of a Confederate blockade runner attacked and destroyed the previous day by a Union vessel.

    Rose was terrified. Knowing that she would be a target and doubtless arrested when the Union crew boarded the stricken ship, she felt that escape to a sympathetic Southern community was her only hope. Seeing that the shore was a short distance away, she demanded that a lifeboat take her there. The captain sternly advised against that in the face of rough water, but Rose was used to having her own way. Finally, she overrode the captain's objections and climbed into a lifeboat with two other passengers who had come aboard in Nova Scotia, Judge James P. Holcombe, the Confederate commissioner to Canada, and Lt. Joseph D. Wilson. They were lowered into the water with two seamen who began rowing toward shore, but the waves were too strong.

    The lifeboat had gone only a short distance when it was caught broadside by a wave and capsized. The weight of the bags of gold sovereigns Rose had tied around her neck, coupled with her heavy black silk dress, prevented her from swimming or staying afloat. Her two companions and the seamen fought the waves and managed to get back to the ship, but there was no sign of Rose. The following morning, her body washed up on the beach.

    It was found there by a Confederate soldier on patrol from nearby Fort Fisher. Upon examining the body and discovering the bag of more gold than he may have dreamed of possessing, he removed it and placed it around his own neck. Then he shoved the body back into the water. Not long after he walked away with the gold, a search party came along the same beach. Once again,

Rose's body was discovered. When the soldier was drawn back by the noise and learned that the woman was a heroine and the gold he had taken was intended for the Confederacy, he felt ashamed. Surreptitiously, he managed to "find" the bag a short distance away in the sand and return it to the proper authorities.

Hidden in the folds of Rose's clothes, the recovery party discovered a copy of her book. Inside was a note for Little Rose, whom she had left behind at the convent:

"London, Nov. 1st 1863. You have shared the hardships and indignity of my prison life, my darling; and suffered all that evil which a vulgar despotism could inflict. Let the memory of that period never pass from your mind; else you may be inclined to forget how merciful Providence has been in seizing us from such a people. Rose O'n Greenhow."

The body was then carried by steamer to Wilmington and laid out with a Confederate flag for a shroud. The next afternoon, Sunday, October 1, 1864, Rose received a full military burial in Oakdale Cemetery, Wilmington, North Carolina. Her coffin was wrapped in the Confederate flag and her grave was decorated with a giant wreath of laurel leaves. An excerpt from her obituary in the *Wilmington Sentinel* reads:

"The ill-fated lady, a passenger in the Steamer *Condor*, which got aground in attempting to run in at New Inlet, was drowned in trying to reach the shore in a small boat, which swamped the 'rips.' On the arrival of the steamer *Cape Fear*, which was appointed to convey the remains to town, she was carried to the chapel, where a guard of honor was stationed at the door.

"It was a solemn and imposing spectacle...On the bier, draped with a magnificent Confederate flag, lay the body, so unchanged as to look like a calm sleeper...She lay there until 2 o'clock Sunday afternoon, when the body was removed to the Catholic Church of St. Thomas. Here the funeral oration was delivered by the Rev. Dr. Corcoran...a touching tribute to the heroism and patriotic devotion of the deceased...

"The coffin...was borne to Oakdale Cemetery followed by an immense funeral cortege. A beautiful spot on a grassy slope overshadowed by wavering trees and in sight of a tranquil lake was chosen for her resting place. Rain fell in torrents during the day, but as the coffin was lowered into the grave, the sun burst forth in the brightest majesty, and a rainbow of the most vivid color spanned the horizon."

Each Confederate Memorial Day, Rose O'Neal Greenhow's grave is decorated by local citizens. But the scene in 2004 when visited by Rose's descendants bore no resemblance to that of October 1, 1864. John O'Neal writes: "It was a muddy mess with trees down, leaves and bark stripped and debris everywhere. We drove through horizontal rain, the remnants of Hurricane Charley, to reach Wilmington. I've been informed the cemetery has been cleaned up and the foliage is recovering nicely, (but) the tranquil lake, mentioned in Rose's obituary no longer exists."

Rose's story did not end with her death. She had left Little Rose at the Sacred Heart Convent, planning to reunite with her at the end of the war. The Convent existed as such until 1919 when it became the Rodin Museum. Official records in the

Archives of the Province of France of the Society of the Sacred Heart in Poitiers indicate that Little Rose remained there only until 1866. A letter to John O'Neal from Sister Duclaux states that no address in Paris was listed for her from the years between 1866 and 1870 when she reached the age of 17, and several accounts state that American friends took her home.

It is known that Little Rose moved in with Florence Moore and her husband, General Treadwell Moore, who was then the Commandant at Newport, Rhode Island. There she met and fell in love with Lieutenant William Penn Duvall, a young West Pointer who was about to embark on a distinguished military career. They were married at Newport, Rhode Island on November 30, 1871. (It should be noted that his surname is the same as the young girl who first thrust Rose into infamy by delivering a message for General Beauregard. If there is a family connection, it is not known.)

Duvall served in the Spanish-American War, in the Philippines, and in the First World War. Along the way, he received numerous honors and decorations, eventually retiring as a General. However, life for Little Rose was not happy. Duvall was known as a severe disciplinarian to the servicemen under him. Apparently his temperament carried over into their home and he accused his wife of "flightiness." The rift and discord between them was such that they were divorced after the birth of their only child, Mary Lee, who was born in New York about 1872.

Her freedom granted, Rose took wing to forge an acting career on the stage. Having grown up in the shadow of her vivacious mother, she surely observed first-hand the frequent amorous situations contrived to extract military secrets. When her husband's rigidity became too much to bear, she may have sought to recapture the fanciful life by plumbing her own theatrical potential. The fact that no reviews have been located detailing the shows in which she appeared suggests that her career was less than luminous.

Apparently Little Rose had little or no contact with her husband or daughter after leaving home. The following wedding announcement in *The New York Times* dated September 19, 1894 mentions the bride's "parents," but lists only her father's name. This along with the society item of Feb. 9, 1906 verify that William Duvall indeed remarried after the divorce:

"Fort Monroe, VA, Sept. 18, 1894. The marriage of Miss Mary Lee Duvall, daughter of Lieut. William P. Duvall of the United States Army, to Louis E. Marie, a son of the late John B. Marie and nephew of Peter Marie of New York, took place today at high noon, in the Star of the Sea Chapel. The ceremony was followed by a breakfast at the home of the bride's parents. The house and church were elaborately decorated with white roses, sweet peas, and asters…Mr. Marie, who is almost as well known in New York as in his native city, is an architect and owns a handsome estate called Brookdale, near Philadelphia."

Further society items follow: *Washington Post* Feb. 9, 1906. Invited to a State reception in honor of the Army & Navy: Maj. & Mrs. William P. Duvall and Mr. & Mrs. Louis E. Marie.

"*Washington Post* April 6, 1916. Mr. and Mrs. Louis E. Marie, of Philadelphia…are among those who are at the Shoreham Hotel.

Little Rose left few clues as to her life after the stage. When that phase of her life faded, accounts indicate that she returned to France and found solitude in religion. The location and date of her death are not known.

Rose O'Neal Greenhow and Little Rose

Photographed by Matthew Brady Studio
at Old Capitol Prison, Washington, DC

1863-1864

REFERENCES

Beymer, William Gilmore, *On Hazardous Service: Scouts and Spies of the North and the South*, Harper and Brothers, 1912, pp. 179-210.

Blackman, Ann, *Wild Rose: Rose O'Neale Greenhow, Civil War Spy*. New York: Random House, 2005.

Farquar, Michael, "'Rebel Rose,' A Spy of Grande Dame Proportions." *Washington Post*, September 18, 2000, p. A1.

Ross, Ishbel, *Rebel Rose*. St. Simon's Island, Georgia: Mockingbird Books, 1973.

O'Neal, John W., II. *My Article.*
http://www.officialwebsite.com/RebelRose/Rose3htm
http://www.spartacus.cschoolnet.co.uk/USACWgreeenhow.htm.

Rose O'Neal Greenhow Papers: Special Collections Library,

Duke University. http://scriptorium.lib.duke.edu.greenhow/

Women in American History: Rose O'Neal Greenhow: Excerpt from *Diary of a Confederate Spy*.
http://search.eb.com/women/pri/Q00176.html

LYDIA KNAPP HORTON
1843-1926

Lydia Maria Smith, born in 1843, grew up comfortably in West Newbury, Massachusetts, a sleepy town north of Boston near the Atlantic Ocean. The sea provided much of the area's livelihood and many a wife or sweetheart left behind stood on the docks at Newburyport searching the horizon for returning loved ones. The fresh salt air and omnipresent seagulls were constant reminders of a wild, beckoning world beyond the confines of the staid New England village.

Lydia especially loved spring when the colorful wildflowers erupted, trees budded, and flocks of small birds newly arrived from distant climes joined the winter residents, the blue jays and cardinals, to diligently construct nests on leafing branches. Along the shore, the wintering mallards and geese saw their coves populated by new waves of herons, plovers, and other opportunists drawn by the abundant fish and crabs.

Lydia's artistic talents, honed by her surroundings, emerged at an early age. Recognizing her potential, her parents arranged for a rich education that included art, music, and good literature. When she was not in class, she could be found seated on the lawn observing nature from every angle. There she put her sketch pad, pen, and chalk to work.

It was not long before her sisters, Helena and Mary Louise, were so taken by her drawings that they begged for lessons as well. Soon all three girls were excelling in watercolor. Lydia had an exceptional eye for shading. She captured flowers and birds in vivid drawings that drew the admiration of her friends and neighbors. She was so appreciative of their praise that she invariably thanked them with the gift of a favorite drawing.

Sometimes Lydia's mind wandered from visible subjects and she drew pictures of imaginary places she dreamed of visiting one day, a dream she shared with seafarers and her own family. Long before she was born, her Grandfather Smith had left home to seek his fortune in California, the new Eldorado so many yearned to visit. The distance and rigors of an ocean voyage in a tiny vessel thwarted most dreamers, but he was not deterred. In 1826, he set off from Newburyport with other hopeful passengers on a small wooden ship.

Months passed before the family learned his fate. The ship survived the treacherous strait around South America, but once it encountered the rough waters of the Pacific Ocean, it was buffeted by one storm after another. Masts cracked, sails were blown away, men were hurled overboard by the gales, and the ship became disabled. Despite heroic efforts by the crew, it sank. Several sailors clinging to floating timbers were rescued by a passing ship, but most, together with the passengers, were lost.

Instead of deterring Lydia's father, Daniel Smith, the loss of his own father on a mission to obtain an ephemeral fortune merely whetted his determination to reach California. Nothing, not even the prospect of never again seeing his wife, Charlotte, and their daughters, was sufficient to thwart his desire.

    Lydia often recalled her terror and heartsick feeling as she stood on the dock at Newburyport clutching her father's coat sleeve and begging him to stay. He smiled at the tearful six-year-old and assured her that he was going to the most beautiful place in the world. He promised to bring back wondrous gifts for her and the entire family, gifts she could not even imagine. She watched as he boarded the brig "Ark" with a large complement of fellow 49ers, each expecting to return with bottomless bags of gold. Blowing a kiss to his loved ones, he turned his face toward the horizon, his eyes on the prize.

    For two years, Lydia, her mother, and sisters awaited his return. They read newspaper accounts and heard secondhand stories of great fortunes, others of lives lost or broken by the laborious search for nuggets. To his family's dismay, Daniel Smith was one of the less fortunate who sought riches in California. In 1851, he returned home with empty pockets and tales of woe. While his labors did not earn the fortune he craved, his hardships forced him to develop useful skills for survival during the time he was away.

By the time he arrived back, the Industrial Revolution was already underway in Massachusetts and there was a demand for a new generation of manufactured tools essential for the new economy. His decision to open a tool shop in West Newbury not only answered that need, but also provided a substantial income to support his family.

At the outset of the Civil War, Lydia was only 17, but she was already a popular young lady in the village. Although her lovely features and accomplishments attracted many eligible young men, her heart went to Frank Fenelon Knapp. Before he left for service, they became engaged. While Frank served in the 25th Massachusetts Regiment, Lydia did everything in her power to help the fighting forces. She went to work with the Sanitary Commission to raise money for their support by knitting clothes, rolling bandages, and undertaking other urgent tasks.

When at last the war ended and Frank returned home, she could not believe her good fortune. Other young women of her acquaintance could not enjoy such a glorious reunion because their fiancés had been killed. As the days wore on, however, it became clear to her that Frank was not well. While serving in North Carolina, he had contracted yellow fever, a dreaded disease with no known cure, and when he died, she thought her life had ended. Instead, a brand new chapter began.

Frank Knapp's older brother William quickly recognized the wonderful qualities Lydia offered and began courting her in earnest. Thirty-seven, a veteran seaman, and never married, he was considered by the women of her family and the town as "quite a catch." He had gone to sea on the brig "Eveline" at seventeen and experienced exotic adventures on duty in the Pacific. His service enabled him to visit the Sandwich Islands and California many times, but when his ship was wrecked on the Columbia River in 1850, he decided to try his luck in the Gold Rush. Like Daniel Smith, he reaped little fortune from two years of toil and returned to sea. Eventually, he became based in

Newburyport and spent the next decade sailing to Canada, Europe, Asia, and South America.

At the start of the Civil War, he enlisted in the United States Navy and was assigned as Acting Ensign to the U.S. McDonough. Barely a year had passed before July of 1863 when his ship was destroyed in battle with Confederate forces at Stone Inlet, South Carolina. He next was ordered to take charge of a battery that shelled Charleston. A commendation for his actions in that post led to a promotion as Acting Master.

At the close of the war, Knapp was assigned to the U.S.S Shallot. Two months after marrying Lydia, then only twenty-two, he was sent to China. The voyage took him to England, Africa, Singapore, and Hong Kong. For his return trip, Knapp was transferred at Hong Kong to the "Wyoming." Instead of retracing the movements of the Shallot, its captain sailed for Boston by way of the treacherous Cape Horn at the southernmost point of South America. Knapp was at last reunited in Newburyport with Lydia and their first son, William Bailey Knapp, who had been born 28 December 1866.

Having completed his naval service, Knapp was detached from the "Wyoming" in February 1868 and honorably discharged in May of that year. For the rest of her life, Lydia enjoyed recounting his adventure in Africa where the picture he carried of her on the journey was stolen from his stateroom. Discovering the loss, Knapp enlisted the aid of some burly sailors and set forth after the thief. They recaptured Lydia's picture in the nearby village and left the culprit ruing his misdeed. Upon Knapp's return, Lydia wrote a brief narration of her husband's adventure on the back of the picture. It would accompany them on still more journeys.

Lydia had grown up with the specter of California hanging over her shoulder. Now that she was married to a man who had been there often and experienced its wonders first hand, she was bursting with desire to see that promised land. Because of her own desires and his new position with the U.S. Engineering Corps, Knapp had little difficulty coaxing her to travel there and make it her home. Their destination was San Francisco where he had been assigned to the Tidal Gauge &

Meteorological Observation Division of the U.S. Coast & Geodetic Survey.

The journey was not easy with a small child and another on the way. They sailed from Boston to Spinal (now Colón), Panama, where they boarded the Panama Railway that had been constructed across the Isthmus to accommodate the surge of adventurers traveling from the East to California during the Gold Rush. Its track, considered a marvel for the time, traversed a rugged 48 miles of terrain before reaching the terminus at Panama City overlooking the Pacific Ocean.

After a brief rest, the family boarded another ship that finally sailed into San Francisco in September 1868, little more than a month from the outset of their trip. They settled into a home at the Presidio, a U.S. military fortification located in a scenic area of rolling hills and abundant nature. It was exactly the kind of place that appealed to Lydia's artistic senses. She had little time to resume her drawing before their second son, Philip Crosby Knapp was born January 15, 1869.

Just as Lydia was beginning to feel at home in San

Francisco, her husband was appointed to the position of Tidal Gauge Keeper at the San Diego station. Barely a year in California had elapsed until September 1869 when they arrived in San Diego on the "Arizona."

Lydia's spirits sank as they disembarked on the wharf at Old Town, a tiny settlement, then only two years old. The scene before them depressed her. She saw only three decent buildings among the squalid, one-story shacks strewn through the brush. She had loved San Francisco and assumed that all California towns were equally enchanting.

William Knapp observed that San Diego had changed little since he spent time there two decades earlier, but nothing he had told Lydia prepared her for disappointment. They spent the first night at Donnell's Hotel, an unpleasant place that had been a faltering attempt by the developer to lure new residents. She was somewhat appeased the next day when they moved into the three-story Franklin House Hotel. The family remained there until their furniture followed them from San Francisco by ship. Lydia's spirits plummeted again during unloading as she watched clumsy handlers drop precious belongings into the bay. It was several days before enough help was hired to retrieve the furniture from the water. The drying out process took far longer.

From the outset, it was vividly clear to Lydia that San Diego offered none of the pleasures or beauty coloring her earlier dreams of California. With two children to tend, she desperately needed space larger than the few rooms the Franklin House provided. Knapp shared her concern and soon located a house built on Point Loma by Louis Rose, a developer with grandiose hopes for Roseville. The town bearing his name occupied the narrow strip of land lying between the San Diego River and the bay.

Relieved though she was to move into a house, Lydia saw no future in the subdivision that was carefully mapped but virtually uninhabited. Gazing in every direction, she saw only desert, scrub brush rustled by the sea breeze, and a solitary dirt road that allowed those inclined to walk or ride a horse, the only means of reaching the lighthouse at the very tip of Point Loma.

Unlike the Presidio, Lydia's new home was not

surrounded by congenial neighbors and inviting nature paths. At the beginning, her nearest human contacts were Chinese fishermen who plied waters along the shore, whalers more likely to be at sea than on their base at Ballast Point, and one Mexican family in La Playa, where Knapp checked the tidal gauge twice daily. The simple technique involved a roll of paper marked by a pencil recording the rise and fall of the tide.

    For lack of little else to do, Lydia and the children often accompanied him on his rounds to La Playa. They took the government launch assigned him from the dock where it was tied up. Lydia always looked forward to the fresh salt air and gently flowing water, a reminder of her childhood. The launch was also essential for their weekly trip to New Town. Residents there were always happy to see a flag being raised atop the lighthouse. This was the signal that a steamer was arriving from San Francisco with the mail.

    Except for the launch that allowed them to connect with the land across the bay, two horses were their only means of transportation for the Knapp family. When their supplies needed replenishing, they rode to the general store in Old Town. There they made the acquaintance of other residents and newcomers who were charmed by Lydia's cultured manners. Soon she and Knapp were invited to attend the frequent banquets and balls planned by fellow settlers eager to expand their friendships and find relief from the lonely days spent in the bleak environment.

In April 1871, Lydia was relieved to move at last into their own home, a small structure Knapp built during a four-month period. Because his job allowed him ample free time, he undertook several projects of this nature, developed an interest in local politics, and became so well regarded by residents of Old Town that they elected him as a delegate to the Republican County Convention.

These friendships proved all the more valuable when Knapp received word in 1872 that his position in San Diego was eliminated. The government had decided that each state and territory would have only one gauge, and since the one in San Francisco would be retained, his would be transferred to the territory of Washington. After much consideration, Lydia and

William decided to remain in San Diego. They both felt certain that he would find an acceptable occupation there.

During the two preceding years, many businesses and government offices had moved from Old Town to New Town. If the Knapps were to benefit from the community, they would have to relocate. Rather than build a second home, they arranged for theirs to be floated across the bay and placed on an ocean-view lot on Front Street.

For the next year, Lydia was in her element. Alonzo Horton, a wealthy San Francisco merchant, and his wife had invested in New Town and made their home there. By the time the Knapps settled into the community, Horton had given five denominations lots on which to construct their churches. In June 1873, he donated a lot to the Unitarians and Lydia immediately joined the group organizing a Unitarian Sunday School. Her capabilities became apparent to the others immediately and they named her first Secretary-Treasurer of the Sunday School.

But just as she was reaping joy and self-esteem from doing something of value for the community, Knapp dashed her dreams by announcing that that the family would move back to San Francisco. Because he had been unable to find a position to his liking in the young town, life at home became stressful. After several attempts, his effort to reestablish connections with friends in the Federal Government was finally fruitful; the offer of employment as a postal clerk in the San Francisco Post Office came at a critical moment and was one he could not reject.

Lydia was devastated. Just as she was becoming a major cog in the civic whirl of San Diego, she was uprooted. She blamed herself for not being more self-reliant. She told herself that if customs were more lenient, she would have remained with the children and let her husband move to San Francisco by himself to test the waters. If the job proved worthwhile, she and the children could then join him. Meanwhile, she would be able to pursue the role she felt destined to play in life.

But social customs did not conform to her wishes. Although she was reluctant to pull up stakes and go to San Francisco, her husband's situation dictated their lives; Lydia realized that she had nothing of consequence to say that would alter his decision. Fortified by happy memories of their stay at the Presidio, she watched their belongings stowed on the "Orizaba," the same vessel that had delivered them to San Diego. Stoically, she boarded it with her husband and sons for the move back to San Francisco.

No sooner did they arrive in October 1873 than Lydia discovered that the pleasant accommodations she had enjoyed at the Presidio were not available to a postal clerk. Instead, they were forced to settle for a less desirable home. With little to love about her situation, she was reminded daily how deeply she missed her friends and her position in San Diego; even more, she yearned to visit her family in Massachusetts. She began dropping little hints to Frank about her wishes. When they did not move him, she protested that her own sanity and health were dependent upon seeing her family.

Knapp was unresponsive to her request. He could not afford the cost of sending an adult and two children on such a long journey. Nothing, not even her adroitly manufactured tears, swayed him. Then the tears became real. Lydia despaired of ever seeing her mother and sisters again until the joyous day when her mother sent her money enough to make the journey by train.

She and the boys, now aged seven and ten, crossed the country in June 1877. The visit would last throughout the summer, exactly what she needed to refresh her spirits and prepare her for the trip back to her husband and San Francisco. Each week she mailed him a cheerful letter about their activities and envisioned a smile crossing his face to know that his family would rejoin him in time for the opening of school in September. But instead of receiving sufficient funds for the return passage, she heard nothing from Knapp. Not one letter.

At last she took it upon herself to contact him through mutual friends. A flurry of letters back and forth convinced her that he had no intention of providing the needed funds. After deep thought and concern for her children, she put the boys in school in Newburyport and notified her husband that she could not justify maintaining their marriage. Their tacit agreement to separate shoved her in a new direction.

Lydia could not pinpoint the exact time she stopped

loving William Knapp. Perhaps it had been in San Francisco when he persistently ignored her urgent pleas to visit her family. Perhaps it was in San Diego when he disregarded her own accomplishments and took the job in San Francisco without consulting her. She wondered if she had ever truly loved him or if he had been merely a substitute for her first love, his brother Frank.

True, life with him had been exciting for a time. He was worldly in more ways than a woman of her restricted upbringing could fathom. She had thrived when he introduced her to California, that magical place of her childhood fancies. For all its warts, it was destined to become an integral part of her life. After all, she argued with herself, William was the father of her sons. Still, she knew the boys would remain closer to her as long as she lived, for they had shared her initial heartache when the marriage ended and rejoiced in her personal achievements and conquest of roadblocks placed by society to thwart women who did not conform to a certain mold.

If Knapp ever changed his mind and pleaded with her to

return to him with the boys, she never confided as much to friends. Nothing in her behavior revealed that she could be induced to waver from her decision. So, freed from the responsibility of tending to an ungrateful husband, she set out to fulfill all the youthful aspirations that had ended with marriage.

Her initial good fortune was funding from her parents who supported her lifelong desire to study art seriously. At first, she attended classes in Newburyport, but her talent was so extraordinary that her instructors urged her to seek advanced courses in Boston.

While her parents supervised the boys and saw them off to school, Lydia commuted to classes several days each week at Cowles Art School, a renowned institution specializing in an open approach to natural subjects. She traveled there by the trains that connected Newburyport and other North Shore towns with the city and quickly began to thrive as she perfected her skills under the tutelage of experts. The encouragement they offered gave her the confidence to open her own art school in Newburyport.

Eager students enrolled in her painting classes. One of her specialties was painting on china, a skill newly popular and in great demand. The technique had been introduced locally during the 18th century by the exquisite Chinese porcelain transported by whalers docking at ports throughout New England. The focus was on scenery and landscapes, subject matter that delighted Lydia and earned endless compliments.

With her art school thriving, she spread her many talents throughout the community. She became an active member in church groups and a variety of women's clubs dedicated to bettering society. One of her foremost passions, the women's rights movement, was served by the Woman's Suffrage Society. As a gifted speaker capable of expressing her opinions in a forceful manner, it is likely that she shared details of her own circumstances to warn other women to prepare for an uncertain future by fortifying themselves with talents and careers in the event of a marital rupture…or spinsterhood.

Lydia flourished as a community leader in Newburyport for more than ten years. During that time, William Knapp died in

San Francisco on June 24, 1885 after suffering a stroke. The small estate he left her and their sons included four lots in San Diego, land he purchased while they lived in Roseville. Two years after the lots were purchased for slightly more than one thousand dollars by E. W. Morse, a family friend, Lydia left the successful life she had cultivated in Newburyport and returned to San Diego. Explanations for her departure were scant, but it was rumored that her primary reason for going was to sort out business affairs.

Upon her arrival, she found an unfamiliar San Diego. During her absence, the population ballooned to more than ten times its former size. But the unexpected changes had not dimmed her reputation. Even though she had been away for many years, old friends remembered her and warmly welcomed her into the community, among them Alonzo and Sarah Horton, the most influential couple in the city's business and politics during its early days. Although there is no record of an on-going correspondence, one can imagine that Lydia maintained contact with her friends in San Diego throughout the time she was away. Did returning there ever figure into her plans? Perhaps not initially, but Knapp's death may have reawakened a spark of interest in the place where she first rose to social prominence.

Lydia soon was placed in charge of the Women's Exchange where handiwork was sold or bartered. A position more to her liking became available at the Southwest Institute when the art teacher resigned from the private school. Her artistic and teaching background made her the ideal candidate to fill the vacancy. She was promptly appointed and settled into a comfortable new life that extended to the Unitarian Church in the role of Sunday School Superintendent.

On November 21, 1890, Lydia's life became even more comfortable. A year earlier, Sarah Horton was thrown from a carriage and killed while visiting in Washington, DC. She was the fourth wife Alonzo Horton lost to death or accident. At age seventy-seven, he could not imagine spending the rest of his days alone, so he soon offered marriage to the active woman so highly regarded for her breeding, wit, intelligence, and charm. Despite the thirty years difference in their ages, Lydia lost no time in accepting the community icon known to all as "Father" Horton. Her duties as mistress of the Horton mansion suited her perfectly. As they began to require her constant attention, she compensated for the lack of spare moments during the day by easing away from teaching. This allowed her to devote herself to painting as a hobby and participate wholeheartedly in local cultural activities.

In 1892, Horton sold the mansion and they moved into a smaller home on State Street with an even better view of the harbor. Happy in his retirement, he became known as San Diego's official greeter. The title well suited the stately, bearded gentleman who spent his days watching ships arrive from San Francisco and hurrying down to the wharf in his carriage to welcome the passengers.

For her part, Lydia was committed to boosting the role of women in society. When some influential local women organized the Wednesday Club to promote artistic and literary culture, she quickly volunteered to be one of the thirty-three charter members. Aware of her abilities and earlier involvement in women's clubs in Massachusetts, the members elected her as their first president. The organization developed into one of the most influential in San Diego and played a substantial role in supporting the local library, children's homes, and other institutions providing outlets for women.

Now that she was in financial circumstances befitting a society lady, Lydia invited her mother to move in with them. Charlotte Smith made the journey from Massachusetts in 1895 and remained with her daughter and son-in-law until her death in 1898. Meanwhile, Lydia's sons visited several times after her marriage to Horton, but they could not disguise their dislike of him. The forced separation from their father at critical ages in their development made them resentful of all men who took an interest in their mother.

At the outset of the Spanish American War, Philip Knapp joined the Volunteer Signal Corps and sailed for Manila with General Arthur MacArthur. To support her sons and all military involved in the fray, Lydia became a publicist and fund raiser for the Red Cross. At the same time, she focused her expertise on the

San Diego Public Library. Upon being elected a member of its Board of Trustees and named Secretary of the Board, she wrote to Andrew Carnegie seeking one of the grants he was giving various American cities for library buildings.

Carnegie was pleased to comply with a donation of $50,000 provided the city agreed to provide the site and maintain the building. It was his first gift to a library west of the Mississippi and when the cornerstone was laid March 19, 1901, Lydia presented a paper detailing its history beginning in 1882 in modest rooms in a local bank building. The new building by those who designed the Congressional Library in Washington was opened in 1902. Lydia was hailed by fellow trustees who attributed the library to her energy and devotion.

For the next seven years, Lydia was active on the library's Board of Trustees and was the founder of its Children's Room. Having raised two successful sons, she felt it her duty to provide the next generation with guidance and a view of the world through books. Her interest in children extended to serving on the Boards of the Associated Charities and the Children's

Home Association and raising necessary funds by devoting her time and talents to their causes.

    Her own situation hit a snag in 1903 when the city of San Diego ceased payment to Horton for Horton Plaza. That loss of income sent Lydia back to work, this time as the Librarian at the State Normal School. Her new job meant that she must spend less time with her civic and social activities. At age 89, Horton remained spry and so interested in San Diego's continuing development that his daily routine was to drive about the city and monitor its progress. He rarely strayed from his schedule until December 1908 when he became so ill that Lydia had him admitted to Agnew Sanitarium. His death at age 95 on January 7, 1909 launched an outpouring from the citizens beyond anything the city had experienced. The largest funeral in San Diego at that time, it was held in Elks' Hall where more than 8,000 friends and admirers visited his casket. After the Masonic services, his body was carried to rest at Mount Hope Cemetery along streets lined with grateful citizens.

    William and Philip Knapp, both living in San Francisco,

attended to be with their mother and help her get through the ordeal. They all expected her to benefit from Horton's estate; to their shock, Horton left no estate. Over the years, he had bought and sold countless properties, but he died penniless except for the home where he and Lydia lived.

Now 66 years of age, Lydia had no option but to continue in her position at the Normal School Librarian, even though she had been contemplating retirement for some time. Within a year, she simply could not undergo the daily grind, so she resigned and sold the house. The proceeds from the sale, together with a monthly contribution of $100 from Philip Knapp, a successful businessman, provided her with the financial support she needed to return to key positions in the Wednesday Club and other cultural organizations.

Among her close friends in the community was Daisy Sheran, the owner of a large Victorian house and a fervent supporter of women's rights. At Daisy's invitation, Lydia moved into the spacious house and together they crusaded for the passage of a law granting woman suffrage in California. Their efforts enabled its passage in 1911.

Following that major accomplishment, Lydia was asked to serve on the Women's Board of the 1915 Panama-California Exposition. They selected a site in City Park to be developed to accommodate the exposition. Today it is known as Balboa Park. Coincidentally, friends in San Francisco invited her to serve as an Honorary Vice President of the Panama Pacific Exposition held in their city. The two events placed her in the limelight as a hostess for both and bestowed her with the honor of entertaining visiting dignitaries.

The entire city looked to Lydia Knapp Horton for leadership. At the outset of World War I, she was named Vice Regent of the San Diego Chapter of the U.S. Service League, an organization to aid servicemen. She became its Librarian, a position that lasted throughout the war. When the first contingent of Liberty Boys left San Diego, she was named Grand Marshal of their patriotic escort to the battleships.

Before the war ended, she purchased a bungalow near her Wednesday Club. There she frequently regaled guests with speeches about San Diego and its growth from her earliest days . She was joined after the war by her son, William, a widower, who became a realtor in the boom town. William's arrival was fortuitous. Shortly after he moved in, Lydia suffered a slight stroke in 1921. Following hospitalization for a few weeks, she was released, but never regained her former vigor. By 1923, it became clear that Lydia could not wend her way about the city on her own and needed special attention, so Helena Smith moved from Massachusetts to care for the older sister who had devoted her life to serving the beauty of nature and the value of mankind.

A year after her sister moved in, Lydia suffered a severe stroke. She remained in St. Joseph's Hospital for nineteen months living for the day when she could return home. She was able to do so shortly before dying on October 17. 1926 at age 83 in familiar surroundings.

The *San Diego Union* hailed her as a pioneer woman destined to be called "Mother" of San Diego because of her good works and contributions to the city and its citizens. Following the funeral, she was buried in the Horton plot near her husband and his former wife, Sarah. Except for small bequests to her sisters, nieces, nephews, friends, and Horton's niece, she left her estate to her two sons.

    Lydia Knapp Horton was uncommon for her day. As a married woman, she could have adhered to custom and submitted to her husband's rule. Instead, she surmounted disappointments, one after another, and made it her business to spread the word and show by example that women have the power to liberate themselves from the roles society expected of them.

Lydia Knapp Horton, 1860
Copyright San Diego Historical Society

REFERENCES

Fuller, Theodore W. Alonzo Erastus Horton in "San Diego Originals," California Profiles Publications, 1987.

MacPhail. "A Liberated Woman in Early San Diego,". Journal of San Diego History, Vol. 27, No. 1, pp. 17-41.

THE WOMEN OF ARIZONA TERRITORIAL ASYLUM FOR THE INSANE 1886-1912

Lily Bell (sometimes spelled Lilly or Lillie Belle) Kellogg Hancock was an unwitting guinea pig for a host of women born a century later. Along with many of her contemporaries, she was subjected to the worst of demeaning situations at the hands of a few prominent men. Foremost among these was her husband, Judge William A. Hancock, hailed by historians as the "father" and founder of Phoenix, Arizona.

To better understand the dire situations in which Lily was

placed throughout much of her adult life, we begin by looking at the Arizona Territory itself and the Territorial Asylum for the Insane, the institution where she spent considerable time. The experiences she underwent may be seen through the stories of some of the other women incarcerated there who were subjected to similar treatment during the same period.

The wide open Arizona Territory was the promised land, the destination of restless pioneers of every stripe: the young, the ambitious, the despairing, the wild, the temperate, the lawless, the opportunist, the daredevil, and the religious fanatic.

By solitary steed, shank's mare, or horse and buggy, they converged upon the Southwest in the late 1800s with curiosity and desire, intent upon carving a future in the desert amid the mesquite and hostile wildlife. For the men, opportunities to succeed were boundless, limited only by personal flaws. Their female counterparts, however, were pawns in a game of jeopardy.

Employment opportunities for women revolved around serving single men in want of cooked meals, clean rooms, laundered garments, and the kind of recreation that only a woman-starved male craves. An occasional spinster teacher or nurse ventured into the Territory, but the bulk of the female population consisted of two opposing camps: respectable matrons and all others. Crammed into the latter category were the servant, the vagrant, the alcoholic, the hardened criminal, the prostitute, and the misbegotten.

No matter their social status, all pioneer women were second-rate citizens, unable to vote, to participate in official projects, or to protect themselves against whatever evil lurked in the hearts of the men closest to them. The wise woman conducted herself with decorum. If married, she tended her household dutifully, obliged her family's needs, and behaved modestly.

Woe be to those who roiled the waters either by design or disposition. The nag, the afflicted, the religious zealot, the depressed, the tippler, and the resentful woman all were burdens to the men they served.

So when the Territorial Asylum for the Insane was

opened in 1886 at the 24th Street and Van Buren Avenue site in Phoenix which it occupies to the present day, many hapless women unable to maintain prudence and a stiff upper lip became cast-off chattels of men craving freedom from financial or emotional responsibility. Like their male counterparts committed to the asylum, some women inmates remained for a lifetime; others survived shorter terms.

While we cannot fathom the unspeakable conditions they endured in the madhouse, the piercing wails coming from adjacent cells, the filth and personal degradation, the official Applications of Commitment for an alleged insane person, housed today in the Arizona State Archives and Public Records Office of the State Capitol, give a tiny window into the trauma and sorrow surrounding the cases heard.

The Application of Commitment to the Territorial Asylum, from its founding until Arizona statehood was achieved in 1912, began with a Complaint. This brief statement outlining reasons for incarceration of an alleged insane person could be submitted to the Probate Court by any aggrieved party, be it a relative, friend, Territory official, or casual acquaintance.

Upon receipt of the Complaint, the Probate Judge, Joseph Campbell during the early years, followed by J. C. Phillips, ordered that the victim be subpoenaed to appear in Probate Court because he or she "by reason of insanity is dangerous being at large." The local sheriff, constable, marshal or policeman was then commanded to arrest the accused forthwith.

Once the individual was apprehended and appeared in court, the Order of Commitment was completed in the matter of a day or two. The Petition, the first of its three main sections, was presented to the court by the accuser. Additional witnesses were called occasionally to support and attest to the symptoms exhibited by the accused.

Next, the subject was examined by two court-appointed physicians who tendered opinions on the patient's competency and general health and completed the Physicians' Certificate of Lunacy. Their affixed signatures signaled the judge to sign the Commitment form. That accomplished, the patient, on order of the Court of Maricopa County, was summarily deposited into the belly of the Asylum.

    Today, many of the victims would be dismissed or their afflictions treated in knowledgeable and socially acceptable ways, often by a prescription enabling them to get on with their lives. But normal body functions were often misunderstood a century ago by both family and physician. Pity the hapless women brought before Doctors R. M. Tafel, H. A. Hughes, or O. E. Plath because of behavior related to pregnancy, the menstrual cycle, or menopause. Many of the medieval opinions these medical school graduates expressed, most likely in agreement with the husband or family member who instigated the commitment, propelled otherwise normal women into a veritable snake pit. A few survived there long enough to be released. Others were not so fortunate.

    Consider the case of Maria de la Bosch, age 22, whose husband, Arthur C., pleaded for her commitment because "she cries frequently and runs away from home at night, often to the canal." Both Arthur and Miss Cruz Parra, who tended Maria, confirmed that the cause of her depression was pregnancy. Upon examination, Dr. Tafel, in company with Dr. W. Warner Watkins, found the patient to be depressed and very quiet. Lack of interest in things about the house was the other factor leading to their decision to commit her on September 8, 1909.

Mabel Dobson, 38, a 20-year resident of the Phoenix Cartwright district, was committed on September 6, 1904 following the successful petition of her husband, Joseph Dobson. He reported that she spoke in a rambling manner, threatened suicide, and suffered from depression brought on by childbirth eleven years earlier. No mention was made of the child. In the presence of the physicians, Mabel sat quietly, "acted morosely," and lamented that she "had sinned and was going to Hell." Upon her entry into the Asylum, she surely understood how true her prediction proved to be.

Julia Barfoot, age 41, moved from New Mexico to 235 North 15th Avenue only two months before Malcolm Barfoot, her husband, complained to the judge that his wife "takes no interest in anything, just sits about all day and refuses to talk." He ventured the opinion that she "seems and acts like she is losing her mind." To support his petition, he brought along Mrs. John Rogers and Mrs. Mary E. Wood, who reiterated his theory. How reliable could these witnesses have been, one wonders, having known Julia for such a brief period?

Dr. Tafel, along with Dr. Louis Dysart, reported Julia to be very quiet with "no interest in sleeping or eating unless food is given and she is told to eat." It appeared to them that she would not talk because she was listening to sounds. She was committed on June 28, 1911 without homesickness being taken into consideration.

Minnie Zion, 31, a Virginia native, had lived in Arizona four years when her husband, P. L. Zion, complained to the courts of her sleeplessness and constant talking while awake. Her conversation, he noted in his petition, was disconnected, moving from one subject to another, mostly religious. Dr. Watkins and Dr. John Thomas concurred that she talked incoherently and constantly. The possible cause, they concluded, was endocarditis (inflammation of the membrane lining the interior of the heart); otherwise, her health was fine. Minnie was committed on

December 21, 1908, just in time for P. L. to celebrate Christmas and the New Year in footloose fashion.

    Lizzie Bowen, 40, suspected that she was being poisoned. The Mesa City resident was born in Germany, but had lived in Arizona for more than 30 years, so the melancholia described by Robert, her husband, was not from having been uprooted from her home. One must wonder if Lizzie's fear of attempted poison grew from aborted attempts by her husband to do away with her. If so, perhaps he resorted to commitment in the Asylum as a legal method of removing her from his life. To support his petition, he declared that she "has fits of violence, tears her clothes, is dangerous to herself, and has requested sufficient medicines given to produce death." Upon examination, Dr. Tafel and Dr. M. W. Breck observed Lizzie's demeanor to be quiet and the condition of her health fair, except for a "loss of flesh" (weight). They observed no signs of the violence her husband reported. Nevertheless, they ordered her committed to the Asylum on March 15, 1906.

    Annie Ellis, age 35, a resident of Arizona for two years

by way of Texas, lived in Tempe with her husband and child. Her part-time work as laundress helped pay for their small house and lot until March 22, 1909, when her husband presented a petition for her commitment because she was "liable to wander away from home." Although he acknowledged that she was not dangerous, he declared that she did not possess sufficient intelligence to care for herself.

The examiners, Dr. R. M. Tafel and Dr. W. W. Watkins, reported that the patient "believes some person is casting an influence on her and makes her weak. She despairs him of the power of doing what she wants to do." They noted that she seemed to be rational, but in ordering her committed, they reiterated the husband's complaint that "she does not take care of house or child and rambles about at all hours of the night." Slightly more than a month later, on May 5, 1909, the "...patient expired at Arizona State Hospital while on conditional discharge."

Minnie J. Blount, age 47, chattered her way into the Asylum. Since their arrival from Illinois six years earlier, she and her husband, F. A. Blount, had lived at 810 North 2nd Street in Phoenix. In his petition, her husband complained, "Minnie talks incessantly and incoherently,...is very nervous,...does not sleep well, and is almost violent at times." The cause, he believed, was mental worry. Doctors Tafel and Hughes, saw scant reaction from her during their examination because "the patient was asleep under influence of hypnosis." However, rather than address the source of her "mental worry," they ordered her committed on December 13, 1909. Exactly one month later, on January 13, 1910, J. A. Kitcherside, Medical Superintendent of the Territorial Asylum, signed a certificate listing the cause of Minnie's death as cardiac insufficiency. Did she smother to death while being held down by attendants?

    Mrs. B. A. Hickman (records do not cite her given name), age 37, moved with her husband to Phoenix from Colorado three years prior to his petition of June 29, 1903. Mr. Hickman reported to Judge Phillips that his wife's mental attacks began three months earlier. At times, he said, she "threatens homicide and tears up the furniture." The cause, he opined, was excessive use of liquid morphine. Judge Phillips, noting that the accused "is irrational at present," sent her to Doctors L. D. Cameron and O. E. Plath for examination. Although they observed nothing unusual in her behavior while in their presence, they ordered her confined. A commentary on the last page of the Order of Commitment notes that no one was capable of paying the expenses of commitment and maintenance in the Asylum. Therefore, no parties were responsible for her during her confinement. Like many other husbands successful in committing a complaining and tearful wife, B. A. Hickman walked out of the courtroom a free man.

Ida Thompkins, 45, may have been experiencing menopause when her husband, George E. Thompkins, and a friend petitioned the court to commit her. It is both curious and ominous that the family friend was Dr. H. A. Hughes, who also served with Dr. Tafel as the examiner in this case. Ida's symptoms, set forth in the petition, were irrational talk, nervousness, and sleeplessness. Because she was in danger of leaving home, she had to be constantly watched. The cause of her problem was listed as "lactation and debility." The doctors reported that Ida had no bad habits, but both found her to be very nervous and restless. While in their presence, she was guilty of "incessant talk." Expressing the belief that Ida was dangerous because she was liable to run away, the committee sent her to the Asylum on May 11, 1905, noting that her husband "has some means" to pay for her commitment and maintenance.

    Anna Anderson Brown, age 39, was born in Sweden and arrived in Arizona four years earlier from Illinois. She and her husband, Jackson C. Brown, lived at the corner of 17th Avenue and Yuma Road in Phoenix. In his petition to commit his wife, Jackson declared that "she has become morbid and on many occasions says and acts without any consciousness of her acts." He added that she was extremely melancholy and of possible danger to others. Dr. Tafel and Dr. H. H. Stone observed that Anna "knew what she was doing, but talked and cried in a nervous manner" during the examination. Her complaint was a desire to visit her sister. They concluded that she was not dangerous to others, but was unable to take care of herself. They committed her on November 25, 1910, without considering that she might be homesick and concerned about family members living elsewhere.

Clara Strong, 32, and her husband arrived in Arizona from Illinois with high hopes. Three years later, on December 23, 1902, E. A. Strong, petitioned the court to commit his wife, citing the morose attacks she suffered during her menstrual periods throughout the previous six years. Although she was not dangerous at large and never threatened homicide or suicide, he testified that she wandered aimlessly about in the house during those periods without eating or sleeping, "talked in a rambling and incoherent manner, and displayed an antipathy toward her oldest girl, whipping her at times very severely and without reason."

Clara was committed two days before Christmas, assuring her husband a worry-free holiday. Four months later on April 4, 1903, Dr. W. H. Ward, Medical Superintendent of the Territory Asylum for the Insane signed a death notice stating that Clara died at the Asylum two days earlier of exhaustion from acute mania.

Maida V. Nielson, age 19, was a single young woman who traveled to Arizona from New Mexico early in 1908 to live with her married sister. Five weeks later, Elijah Allan, her brother-in-law, had endured enough of her presence to petition the court for her commitment to the Asylum. He declared that she "is very absent-minded, cannot carry on a long conversation, refuses at times to eat, and would wander off and become lost if not watched." These traits he attributed to cessation of her menses three years earlier, a trauma caused by her father, whom he regarded as a "peculiar man, studying and thinking abnormally on religious subjects."

Dr. Clarence Watkins and Dr. Roy E. Thomas conducted the examination. They reported that Maida "speaks slowly with hesitation, does not recall familiar facts, such as family history, and thinks certain foods cause her to receive revelations." They found her to be quiet and orderly and cited "gradual deterioration of her memory and intellectuality" as major factors for ordering her to be committed to the Asylum.

The Maricopa County medical examiners, who attributed some typical behaviors of pregnant and menstruating women to insanity, failed as well in in their assessment of those with true physical ailments. Sadie Vaughn, age 33, a resident of Wickenburg for seven years, was arrested and held in the county jail by Special Deputy Ike Ford. His petition to commit her cited an attack of "nervous prostration" that began a week earlier. He stated: "She has no mind of her own, talks in an irrational manner, and is subject to fits of complete collapse." Dr. L. C. Toney and Dr. J. M. Swetman pronounced her "very filthy, noisy, and slightly maniacal," adding, "...(she) appears to be an epileptic." They ordered Sadie to be committed on February 4, 1905.

Like Sadie, Ola May Farley was an epileptic. A resident of 800 S. Center Street in Phoenix, Ola May was delivered to her doom by her own father's petition, which stated that she threatened to kill herself and others, possessed an uncontrollable temper, and had epileptic fits. Her examiners, Doctors L. D. Cameron and H. Beauchamp, found her to be in good physical condition, clean, and quiet. They noted that she answered all questions put to her, but committed her on December 3, 1906, citing her "inability to remember things, such as the narrow escape of shooting her mother." No particulars were given of that event.

    Dolores Latusmado, age 29, was brought before the court by a petition from Deputy Sheriff Oscar Roberts who testified that she arrived from Mexico a year earlier and worked as a domestic. He placed her in the county jail because she "is an epileptic, is not all right, will not care for her children, and does not sleep." Doctors A. C. O'Connor and Dr. J. W. Thomas noted during their examination that she "does not answer questions intelligently." Could her language have been a barrier? Other reasons for the doctors' recommendation to commit her were "epileptic attacks about once a month," her tendency to become "hysterical at mention of husband or children," and her constant crying. Dolores entered the Asylum on February 1, 1904. The court order assigned no one the responsibility for her maintenance. Did anyone in authority seek to locate her husband

and children? Were they aware that she had been apprehended?

Cordelia Ivy, age 23, was the subject of a petition by her father. He attributed her habit of wandering away from home and talking in an irrational way to attacks that had been ongoing for fifteen years. After identifying himself in the court papers as the graduate of an incorporated medical college, Dr. L. D. Cameron jotted down his suspicion that Cordelia "seems to be deaf." He noted additionally that "she does not seem to understand all that is said to her (and) has fits of temper during which she attacks members of the family or others and attempts to do them violence." Cordelia was committed in early 1903 without receiving help for her deafness. Like others suffering from that affliction, she most likely spent the rest of her days in confinement.

Gracie Wupperman, age 17, was a victim of the nebulous ailment men of the day labeled "nervous prostration." She lived in Yuma with her father, H. Wupperman, who petitioned for her commitment because of her "hysteria, nervous prostration, and general breaking down." During their examination, Dr. L. E.

Taney and Dr. J. M. Swetman noted that she "talks incessantly... and thinks her father is losing his mind and needs looking after." Could Gracie have been the sane family member? No matter, her father had means and was willing to pay her expenses, so the doctors ordered her committed on July 28, 1904.

    Sarah Baker, age 27, had lived in Arizona from the age of three and was married to Edwin Baker, a resident of Tucson. Sarah, however, lived in Commercial Hotel in Phoenix at the time her father, Jesus Figuerra, a resident of Pima County, petitioned the court for her commitment. On June 20, 1910, he stated that she talked irrationally and wandered about, refusing to sleep or eat. The cause, he believed, was spiritualism. Dr. Tafel and Dr. Grant Monica found her to be very quiet, her talk incoherent. They said that she "believes she hears and sees spirits." No evidence was given in the report to equate her behavior to abuse from her husband or others.

    While many Maricopa County men discovered that commitment in the Territorial Asylum was a convenient way to rid themselves of an irritating and unwanted wife or other female relative, Maggie Black, 36, was among those sent to their doom by meddling friends. And all because she suspected her husband of indiscretions while he was away from home working at Mammoth Mine in Pima County.

William Dohency, who identified himself as a friend of the accused, testified that Maggie, a resident of Phoenix for 22 years, "talks incoherently at times (and) imagines people are after her to rob her of her papers and ranch." His belief that she was not able to take care of herself belied his description of the considerable effort she put into maintaining her ranch and tending to her children while her husband was working out of town. During their examination, Doctors Tafel and Hughes reported that Maggie talked about her children, and displayed "muscular twitching, want of coordination, and slow comprehension." They recorded her account of seeing fire in the house and expecting her ranch to burn and her children to be killed, all brought on because she suspected that "her husband is untrue." Even after concluding, "...in our opinion this is temporary," the doctors committed Maggie on April 26, 1906, giving no indication how long she would remain away from her children and ranch. That allowed her husband additional time and opportunity to carouse.

Louise Miller, age 33, was a patient in Sister's Hospital for an unrelated ailment when a friend, Charles E. Hazelton, petitioned for her commitment. The problems consuming her, he declared, were incoherent talk, her wish to get away from those taking care of her, nerves, and poor sleep habits. The cause of these symptoms, he stated, were worry and fear of her divorced husband. Dr. Tafel and Dr. F. G. Augeny reported that the patient talked in an incoherent way, was nervous, prayed, and "walked about combing her hair, drinking large quantities of water, and speaking of things she saw." If Louise was afraid of being stalked by her ex-husband, she need not have worried, for the doctors put her out of his range by committing her on December 16, 1909.

Ruby Dopp, 24, moved to Arizona from Texas at the age of two and had married and given birth to two children by the time J. H. Baker, identified only as "a relative," petitioned the court to commit her to the Asylum. This was necessary, Mr. Baker declared, because Ruby was liable to wander away and do injury to herself and others. During her attacks, he wrote, "she claims her husband is coming for her when, in fact, her husband has not seen or sent for her for more than a year." Mr. Baker did not know the cause of the attacks, but thought they probably were triggered by her husband's abuse.

During their examination of Ruby, Doctors Tafel and Hughes observed that "the patient has hallucinations and is at time incoherent…She has two children, but is unconcerned about them at times and will not let the baby nurse without much trouble. She thinks her husband is coming after her and holds conversations with him although he is not present."

Ruby's depression, brought about by an abusive and absent husband and the responsibility of raising her two young children by herself, would be understandable and treatable today on out-patient basis, but on July 13, 1906, she was committed to the asylum.

Next to women depressed by unhappy marriages or

"female troubles," widows and elderly women (40 and up) were especially vulnerable. Add an arcane religious affiliation and delusions of grandeur, and the outcome was inevitable.

Amelia Darrow, 52, arrived in Phoenix from Joplin, Missouri in late 1911. A widow in excellent health and a fervent follower of Spirit Pilot, a small religious sect of the period, she was bent on doing good wherever fate took her. Deputy Sheriff William H. Woolf petitioned for her commitment after finding her at four in the morning on January 14, 1912 "coming south on 3rd Avenue praying and talking irrationally to herself." She told him she was "chosen by the Odd Fellows and Masons to save this city from destruction." Dr. Tafel and Dr. L. D. Dawson reported that she was somewhat nervous and talkative throughout their examination. She chatted about being rich with a fortune in England and claimed to have a buckle to prove her royal descent. Her conversations with the doctors and with herself were about "money, religion, and Masonry." Despite her claims of wealth, Amelia was found by the court to have no means. Lacking intervention from her son, Fred Darrow of Cartersville, Missouri, she was committed to the Territorial Asylum on January 15, 1912, a few weeks before Arizona achieved statehood.

Carrie List, 50, a resident of Lower Buckeye Road seven miles west of town, was the subject of two separate commitments, the first on February 3, 1904. After taking poison and threatening to kill her husband, she was removed to the county jail while her son, John List, petitioned the court. He attributed her attack to "irritation in home life." Dr. C. A. O'Connor and Dr. John W. Foss reported that Carrie was nervous and confessed to making great effort to control herself from impairing her husband when irritated. They also noted her "tremendous good appearance." Basing their decision on her threat to take the life of her husband, her attempted suicide, her habit of "exposing her person while having an attack," and the promise of relatives to bear all expenses of her commitment and maintenance, they sent her to the Asylum.

Carrie List was committed second on November 18, 1905 following the petition of J. Holley, a friend. He said that she "is excitable and talks insane. She imagines she is given drugged coffee to break her habit of cigarette smoking." All clues point to Carrie's despair from overwork and family behavior. Citing her claim of maltreatment, Mr. Holley reported that she "has left home and refuses to return." He expressed astonishment at her threat to "throw her mother-in-law out of the house and use force if necessary." Doctors Tafel and Swetman did not bother to investigate Carrie's lament that she was saddled with a mother-in-law from hell, although they made note of her declaration that she was abused at home and not tolerated as she should be. They pronounced her "erratic and very talkative." Perhaps she behaved that way because their examination offered the only opportunity to release the ire bottled inside toward her over-bearing husband, children, and the elderly in-law whose constant presence and carping drove her to despair.

  Mary Donnelly, 33, a widow recently arrived from Texas, was staying in a Phoenix lodging house when its residents delivered her to the county jail for complaining that a fellow boarder was trying to kill her. In his petition, Constable Henry Proops said that Mary spoke in an irrational manner and was dangerous to be at large. Doctors Taney and Swetman noted Mary's good physical condition, cleanliness, and temperance. However, they labeled her belief that a man in the lodging house wanted to kill her an "insane delusion" because "reliable witnesses say that no person in the house wanted to kill her." The court made no effort to determine if a resident of the rooming house actually did approach Mary with murder, or something else, on his mind. To ascertain that Mary did not return to her lodging house and claim unwanted advances from another tenant, the court sent her away on March 30, 1905 to cope with the terrifying behavior of the asylum inmates.

Rowena Crafts, age 46, was taken to jail by Deputy Sheriff J. D. Adams, who petitioned the court for her commitment based on her excessive concern for the welfare of her children. He reported, "…she wanders around town annoying people, saying her two children are sick. All physicians say they aren't." Adams feared that she "is liable to give her children poison thinking it is medicine" because she "has a trunk and house full of medicines of all kinds." Dr. Tafel and Dr. H.

Beauchamp examined Rowena, who protested to them that "she was as sensible as any other person." The patient, they noted, "seems to be excited and nervous and over-anxious about the health of her children. She continually seeks advice of doctors." What, one wonders, became of the children when their mother was removed from the picture on July 15, 1904?

Hattie Cranston, age 68, was the subject of a petition by her husband, along with Mr. P. T. Edson, and Rosebeth T. Edson. (The papers do not explain if the latter two were relatives or friends of the accused.) The reasons given were Hattie's "queer ideas concerning her husband" and a threat to take her own life. The probable cause of attack recorded in the order was worry, followed by three hemorrhages of the brain. Dr. A. B. Nichols found Hattie to have a "loss of memory and delusions that some are attempting to kill her husband." He stated that she "answered all questions and seemed to be in good mental condition, with the exception of loss of memory." No matter, Hattie was committed on September 7, 1906.

Sarah Hutchinson, 64, was one of the few women who

received a reprieve from Doctors Tafel and Plath, two of the court-appointed physicians whose recommendations often reflected their lack of knowledge about the female constitution. The petitioners, Sarah's five daughters, appeared in court on March 18, 1909 determined to commit the mother whom they regarded as their adversary.

Mrs. G. J. Murphy, Mrs. A. J. Tweed, Mrs. M. M. Bell, Mrs. M. P. O'Brian, and Mrs. A. H. Hamer testified that Sarah "imagines her children are conspiring to rob her of all she has… She has a great hatred for her own children…She does not eat proper food and becomes so angry she loses control…She has told her friends to look out because it's dangerous to be at large."

Whatever transpired during their examination convinced the doctors that Sarah had good reason to dislike her daughters. Their report was brief and to the point: "In our judgment, she is not insane, not dangerous, and should go at large."

Sarah's reprieve, confirmed on March 30, 1909 by Dr. William Wylie, spokesman for the medical examiners of Maricopa County, came from a Mrs. Morrison, not otherwise identified. While Dr. Wylie's opinion wavered between the original petition and his colleagues' report, he allowed Sarah's conditional freedom. His memo read in part: "We agree she is insane and a menace to self and others, but not sufficiently so to warrant committing her to the Arizona Territorial Asylum…We would commit her there if there was a place fit to care for her. There being no such place and Mrs. Morrison proving to be responsible for her conduct and to see she was properly cared for and protected, we do not commit her to aforesaid Territorial Asylum."

LILY BELL HANCOCK
1855-1943

Like the foregoing women, most proposed for the Territorial Asylum for the Insane were mere blips in society during Arizona's march toward statehood. Unlike them, Lily Bell Hancock was in a loftier league. Married to a highly acclaimed husband, she played a prominent role in local history. Were it not for the extant court papers, her treatment at the hands of an impatient family and an arguably cruel and heartless husband would be undocumented.

Lily Bell Kellogg was born in Crown Point, Indiana, September 15, 1855, the third child of Benjamin William

Kellogg and the former Mary M. Clark. One year later, the family journeyed by covered wagon to Monterey, California. During their stay of nearly 15 years, six more children were born. By the time Lily had reached the age of 15, the family had grown discontented with their prospects in California. In characteristic pioneer style, the entire Kellogg family mounted their horses and began the long journey across mountains and desert to the Salt River Valley, arriving during October of 1871. Lily's father quickly purchased land on Van Buren Street between 12th and 16th Streets, a prime location then as it is today. The farm he developed there thrived until he became bedridden following an accidental fracture of a femur. The subsequent lung congestion led to his death February 14, 1888. Both he and his wife, Mary, who had died the previous year on January 4, 1887 are buried in the Pioneer and Military Memorial Park.

On February 3, 1873, two years after the Kelloggs settled in Phoenix, Lily Bell married William Augustus Hancock. Each may have regarded the other as "quite a catch," in the parlance of the day. Hancock was then 42, considerably older than his 18-

year-old bride, whose very name suggests that she was a fetching beauty, a fresh and genteel face in contrast with the painted ladies of the night and weary household drudges who comprised much of the Valley's early female population. Hancock already had made his mark as one of the commissioners of the Salt River Town Association and administrator of the Phoenix settlement. Securing Lily's hand was one more accomplishment.

Hancock was born May 17, 1831 in Barre, Worcester County, Massachusetts where the Hancock and Lee (maternal side) families had lived since before the Revolution. After completing his education in the local public schools and Leicester Academy, he took over the management of his father's farm. Unlike his ancestors, he yearned to discover what lay beyond New England. At age 22 he could wait no longer.

With two of his brothers, John and Henry, he traveled to Iowa on the first leg of a cross-continent journey. There they purchased 275 head of livestock and supplies for the venture. Driving the cattle before them, they crossed the plains to Sacramento, California. For eight years, they achieved their goal of making a fortune in ranching, raising horses and cattle for the markets.

Shortly before his father's death in 1857, Hancock traveled back to Massachusetts by way of the Isthmus of Panama. After settling the estate, he returned to California the same way, bringing along more horses. He remained on his ranch until the Civil War trickled westward to California by 1864. That November, he volunteered for the Seventh California Infantry and was in Fort Yuma by February, 1865. There he transferred to the Arizona troops and mustered in as second lieutenant in Company C, First Arizona Volunteers on September 1, 1865. At his next station, Fort McDowell, he was promoted to first lieutenant on June 20, 1866. Within less than three months, he mustered out as captain on September 13, 1866.

Instead of returning to his California ranch, he heeded the opportunist within and remained at the fort to become superintendent of its government farm. Later, riveted by the potential of the desolate Arizona desert, he took the responsibility of post trader at Camp Reno, lured by the potential of the desolate Arizona desert.

Hancock's vision became a reality in 1870. Utilizing his knowledge of surveying, he laid out a brand new town ninety-six blocks long and a half-mile wide. By the fall of 1871 he had even built his own adobe house at 33 S. First Avenue, the first building erected in the city of Phoenix.

Ambitious to a fault, Hancock then headed for the fast track, first capturing the position of city postmaster. Shortly after his marriage, he was elected Maricopa County Surveyor and became responsible for surveying the Grand Canal, the Utah Canal, and the Arizona Canal to satisfy the thirsty newcomers. He was admitted to the bar in 1874, the first step toward becoming one of the territory's most successful attorneys. His upwardly mobile career moved steadily forward to probate judge, the assistant to the U. S. Attorney, and the first sheriff of Maricopa County.

Hancock's prestige and aggressive personality might have subdued another young wife, but Lily was not intimidated. As one of the city's most distinguished matrons, she was expected to set an example of subservience, revering her husband while remaining in his shadow. Hancock, however, was dealing with a woman who had taken her arduous journey to the Valley in stride. The daughter of a dreamer whose mastery of the desert was represented by the large farm he cultivated on what is now West Van Buren Street, Lily was a bright, personable woman in her own right. She was not content to play the mousy wife and doting mother.

The 24-year age difference between Lily and her prominent husband may have precipitated the family strife that pricks through the documented past. He settled into middle age just as she blossomed socially and creatively. And while his money and power supplied the basics and the frivolous wants of his young wife, this was not ample consolation for Lily, whose mental anguish, masked by her spunk and inner fire, propelled her across forbidden lines.

Perhaps she was resentful of the time William Hancock spent away from home in the company of the movers and shakers of the political kind, excluding her from his travels. During his absences, she was expected to be the model wife serving tea in the parlor and staying discretely out of the limelight. This was not her style. Spurred by the successful ventures of her husband and his colleagues, Lily yearned to make her own mark in the business world and achieve recognition for accomplishing myriad good deeds. To her misfortune, some were the products of her fertile mind.

On January 14, 1886, two of her husband's associates went before Judge Joseph Campbell to present a petition requesting that Lillie (sic) B. Hancock, then only 31, be committed to the Territorial Asylum. Why did Hancock enlist their services rather than face the court himself?

As a sitting judge, his move was both prudent and officially correct, but behavioral psychology offers two other possible explanations: love and shame. If Hancock stayed away from the courtroom because of his deep love and devotion to Lily, perhaps he believed that presentation of the petition by a third party would allow her to think better of him in the future. On the other hand, his reluctance to appear may have reflected his shame and the belief that marriage to a woman whose bizarre behavior called into question his own good judgment could sabotage his professional career. The testimonies by Louis H. Chalmers and Charles A. Givens were the initial steps in a case that must have set the tongues of Phoenix socialites and the business community wagging nonstop.

Testimony of Louis Chalmers

"I have known Lillie for about a year. Up to the past two weeks, so far as I know, she was sane. During the past two weeks, she has labored under various mental hallucinations, calling at my office frequently and asking me to transact various business matters that were absolutely improbable, and at other times she wished me to transfer all of her property to get money to assist friends… She stated that the parties to whom she wished to convey did not want the property, but that she would make them take it. She talks wildly on various subjects… She would leave with me business to attend to, but the next time I see her would have no recollection of the matter."

Testimony of Charles A. Givens

"I have known Lillie the last four or five years, being the wife of my partner, Judge Hancock. I know her to be an exceedingly quite amiable and modest woman of more than ordinary intelligence and character. Within the last few weeks, I have met her often and she has shown a very marked condition of insanity. She has come to talk about some business affairs talking very wildly and insisting upon certain things and speaking in a low tone and manifesting great excitement…Whenever she could do, she would get a horse and buggy or go out on foot in the daytime and at unreasonable hours of the night without the company of friends and going whenever she could do so by herself…During the absence of her husband a little while ago… her condition was such, and such fears were entertained by her friends that she was kept under constant surveillance and I was compelled to recall her husband while he was engaged in important business abroad. Once during this time, I was reliably informed, she procured a pistol and threatened to use it upon some persons unless they gave up to her a bottle of whiskey in their possession. I was informed that the pistol was taken from her by her brother-in-law by force. I am sure she is at any time liable to do herself or others injury unless restrained. I have seen her the last few weeks and it is apparent to me she is more and more insane every day."

Mr. Givens' testimony gives no insight into Lily's reason for pursuing the bottle of whiskey. Did she crave it herself? That is extremely doubtful. In 1881, the Women's Christian Temperance Union (WCTU) organized in Arizona and began a vigorous campaign against alcohol and saloons. As one of the town's most prominent women, it is quite likely that she was at the forefront of its efforts to rid the city of drunks.

Upon her apprehension and appearance before the court, Lily was examined by Dr. O. L. Mahoney and Dr. O. J. Thibode. They reached three conclusions:

1. We testify that she is insane.
2. It is dangerous for her to go out at large by reason of insanity.
3. That said insanity is likely to prove permanent.

In response, Probate Judge Joseph Campbell gave an order on March 23, 1886 that must have chilled the vivacious Lily to the bone: "I do hereby order that she be delivered into the custody of her husband, William A. Hancock, to be by him placed where she may be properly treated and cured, subject to the order of the Board of Supervisors."

Where did Hancock send his wife? The unfortunate lady became one of the very first inmates of the spanking new Territorial Asylum for the Insane. No private account of her stay has surfaced and the current staff guard their records with zeal.

Lily's confinement came on the heels of a deed Hancock conveyed to her on February 27, 1886 for a homestead property not exceeding $4,000 in value. It launched a financial brouhaha that was not settled until May 13, 1901 in the U.S. Supreme Court case of Luhrs v. Hancock {George H. N. Luhrs v. William A. Hancock, Lilly (sic) B. Hancock, and Thomas W. Pemberton}.

During the course of the court trial, William Hancock was called on April 8, 1898 to testify by Mr. Armstrong, attorney for the plaintiff.

Q. You say you were living on this property and made your home there?

A. Yes.

Q. And you continued to make your home there until you turned it over to Mr. Pemberton in 1886?

A. Yes, that was the home of my family.

Q. Didn't you make your home there with your family?

A. I suppose I called it my home, yet I was not living there all of the time. I called it the homestead of my family; I lived on the other side of the river a part of the time.

Q. When did you commence to live on the other side of the river?

A. Some time in 1889 or '90. I am not certain about that.

Q. Where did your family reside during the time you were residing on the piece of land across the river?

A. My wife was a part of the time here on the homestead and a part of the time in California. One of the children was there in California, although only for a while, and then went back here, and one remained there until she came back here.

Q. The house, all of the time, was occupied by some member of your family?

A. I had a room in it that I occupied some times and a part of the time it was rental.

Q. How much of the time did your wife live here at this house after you went across the river to live, as you say?

A. It is pretty hard for me to say now.

Q. Isn't it a fact that she kept the house open and cared for the children that they might go to school here in the city?

By the Court: What is the purpose of this?

By Mr. Armstrong: It is for the purpose of showing that while he was living there she was claiming a home here and living in California.

Defendant objects to the question as immaterial.

The Court: I don't see that it makes any difference whether they lived there or not, as long as they made a Declaration of Homestead. It was no homestead after 1887.

By Mr. Armstrong: This offer is to show that it was his

intention to make another declaration and to go over there and to claim a homestead for himself.

The Court: The question of homestead is eliminated from this, unless in 1888 there was a homestead so as to determine the validity of this deed. Your points and view of the matter differ. The defendants take the view that because it was a homestead the question of the indebtedness of Mr. Hancock at that time cuts no figure, because the property was exempt from execution and he could part with it as he saw fit to his wife; and your contention is that it does make a difference. The fact that he was in debt himself makes this deed to his wife a fraud, notwithstanding it was a homestead.

By Mr. Armstrong: That is it.

By Mr. Ainsworth (Attorney to the Defendant): That is it exactly.

Q. Did either you or your wife ever make or file any declaration of homestead after July 1, 1887?

A. No. We never filed any declaration of homestead, neither myself nor my wife.

By Mr. Armstrong: I think we will ask a certain line of questions which under our view of the case...

The Court (interrupting): ...that is a matter of defense.

By Mr. Armstrong: When was your wife first adjudged insane?

Defendant objects to the question as immaterial, incompetent and irrelevant, and it cannot be raised in this issue.

No ruling.

Q. Your wife Lily B. Hancock has been insane, has she not?

Objected to as against the defendant, being irrelevant.

Objection sustained.

It was thereupon stipulated between counsel that the following evidence might be offered: that on the 23rd day of March 1886, Lily B. Hancock, the defendant in this case, was adjudged to be insane by a decree of the Probate Court of this County; the plaintiff offers in evidence page 99 of the said Insane Record.

After further questions and objections, another question was asked:

Q. State whether or not your wife Lily B. Hancock was insane and continued to be insane from the 21st day of March, 1883 down to and including the year 1895?

More objections preceded the cross-examination of the plaintiff until the court adjourned.

The opinion ultimately delivered by Justice McKenna May 13, 1901 acknowledged that the said real estate was formally sold to the plaintiff Luhr on February 4, 1893 a year after William and Lilly borrowed for a mortgage that was subsequently foreclosed and purchased by Thomas W. Pemberton. When Pemberton became the purchaser at the foreclosure sale, he received the sheriff's deed for said premises on February 14, 1895, took possession thereof from the Hancocks, and has since paid the taxes and made valuable improvements upon the property. The plaintiff Luhrs was never in possession of the premises.

Among the exceptions tied to the ruling were "the rejection of evidence of the insanity of Mrs. Hancock at the time she executed the mortgage…(and) the admission in evidence of the note and mortgage over the objection of the plaintiff claiming Mrs. Hancock insane and incompetent to make them."

The judge responded that the court did not hesitate to hold such conveyances valid (even though) "the exceptions to testimony were based on the alleged insanity of Mrs. Hancock when she executed the note and mortgage...The deed of an insane person is not absolutely void; it is only voidable; that is, it may be confirmed or set aside."

As we read between the lines of the court proceedings, we learn that William and Lily Hancock lived apart during much of their marriage, possibly until William's death in 1902, just a year following the conclusion of the court case. Did he send her to the Territorial Insane Asylum because of a mental condition? Or was his decision a singular act of cruelty?

During his testimony, William mentioned that Lily spent time in California. Can one infer that he was referencing time she was there for medical, rather than social, reasons?

We do not know how long Lily spent at the Arizona facility; that information is secreted in their files. However, we do know that she spent time in a California facility at least twice prior to 1904, as evidenced by her son's testimony and her admission papers dated May 22, 1904.

How might Lily have traveled to California? In 1893, the Southern Pacific main line ran from El Paso, Texas to Los Angeles via Tucson and Yuma. The only way to leave Phoenix by rail was to take the Arizona and Eastern Railway from Phoenix to connect with the Southern Pacific at Maricopa. There one could board the Southern Pacific en route to Los Angeles.

It was a bit more complicated to reach the Atchison Topeka & Santa Fe Railroad, the main line from Chicago to Los Angeles. All main line trains stopped at Ash Fork west of Flagstaff. To reach that station, a person headed for Los Angeles would have to take a stage coach to Prescott and from there a branch line to Ash Fork. Whichever option Lily and those accompanying her chose, it was not possible to leave Phoenix by comfortable and rapid means. Nevertheless, the arduous journey may have been preferable to remaining in town subjected to rumors and the strict discipline of her aging husband.

In studying the various asylum options California offered at the time Lily was there, it appears that the best choice by far was the brand new Agnews Insane Asylum in Santa Clara, near San José. Established in 1885 by the California State Legislature as a neuropsychiatry institution for the care and treatment of the mentally ill, it opened in 1889. Its innovative architecture and modern methods set it apart from the traditional institutions for the mentally ill.

It is unfortunate that the exact nature of Lily's illness is shrouded. There are numerous possibilities, including postpartum depression, menopause, and simply the despair of marriage to a man who, for whatever reasons, was absent from her home while making his "across the river." Was he supporting another woman? This is not beyond reason. As a key figure in Phoenix business and politics, he walked the tightrope between polite society and the urge to dispose of a troublesome wife.

Upon learning of the new facility in California, he may have viewed the distance beneficial and a way to escape local gossip. After all, when a married woman journeyed to California during the late 1800s, it inevitably was to visit relatives and friends. Who in the town could know that Lily undertook the trip for reasons of insanity?

She actually may have spent several days or weeks visiting friends in Los Angeles before heading northward on the Southern Pacific Railroad. A surviving note from a friend suggests that she may have done so at either the beginning or end of her treatment.

Her destination was nothing like the grim facility with spooky, Charles Addams-style turrets abandoned to make way for a modern building that still stands in the same location near Phoenix's Sky Harbor Airport. It was a charming group of light, airy buildings of Mediterranean Revival style with tile roofs and decorative accoutrements. The large treatment building survived the 1906 earthquake and is today the center of the Sun Microsystems complex in Santa Clara. From the beginning, Dr. Edmund T. Wilkins, the Superintendent, insisted that his progressive mental hospital be designed as a cheerful oasis surrounded by gardens, palm trees, and lawns where the patients could relax.

By 1882, passenger trains regularly ran from Los Angeles to Redding via Oakland. If Lily was admitted to Agnews late in the decade, she would have discovered it to be conveniently accessible via a short ride on the Central Pacific Railroad which also terminated in Oakland. Upon arrival, Lily would have marveled at the lavish grounds kept attractive by gardeners. Fragrant honeysuckle perfumed the buildings that gave way to pleasant walkways, arbors and even croquet grounds. Beyond the fruit trees and vegetable gardens, livestock roamed. It was indeed an estate fit for royalty. One hopes that Lily found peace there far from her overbearing husband.

Regardless of how benign Lily's treatment was, the experience could not help destroying what fondness she may have initially felt for William Hancock, whose public esteem belied his treatment of her. The chill between the couple must have persisted for the rest of his life. With two separate homes, it was an estrangement neither could hide from their children, Harry Lee, the first white child born in the Arizona Territory, and

Mabel, both approaching their teens at the time of their mother's commitment. If she expressed herself in letters or notes passed down to descendents, such memoirs are not among preserved family papers.

On March 24, 1902, William Augustus Hancock died unexpectedly in Phoenix at the age of 71. He was buried in the Knights of Pythias Cemetery, one of seven historic cemeteries in use between 1884 and 1914 that today comprise Pioneer & Military Memorial Park at 15th Avenue and West Jefferson Street, near the Arizona State Capitol complex in Phoenix.

Lily was only 47 at the time of her husband's death. She may have believed that her troubles were over.

By the time her son, 30, appeared in court two years later to request that his mother be committed, Lily had been in and out of the Arizona Asylum three times. The symptoms Harry L. Hancock presented were similar to those given prior to her initial stay. He testified before the court that his mother threatened members of the family and would not allow them to care for her.

"She imagines she has a large amount of business to

attend to, but in reality, she has not," he said.

He offered no reason for his mother's attack, but likened it to five previous attacks, the most recent one occurring six weeks earlier. The doctors evaluated her as rational, noting that she did nothing unusual in their presence. Nevertheless, on May 22, 1904, Lily was again ordered confined in the Territorial Asylum for the Insane.

Two years later, at age 50, she was back in court, subject of another petition by her son. Her symptoms that commenced four weeks earlier, he said, were "erratic conversation and annoying people." Harry L. Hancock feared that his mother was liable to wander away and get lost if not properly restrained.

The court physicians reported that Lily said very little during their examination, merely enough to lament her neglect and ill-treatment. In their summary of her behavior, they noted that she "…writes letters to her friends, then abuses them, is not truthful to her family, and imagines she has great business ability and lots of property to handle." After penning the notation that Lily's son, Harry L. Hancock, would be responsible for her expenses, the judge ordered her committed to the Territorial Asylum for the Insane at Phoenix on June 30, 1906.

Arizona State University houses the Hancock Family Collection, four boxes of manuscripts, newspaper clippings, maps, and 54 folders of papers summarizing the lives and work of the immediate family. Among the collection are reports by Hancock regarding his irrigation projects, and miscellaneous papers describing life in early Phoenix.

There is interesting correspondence between Lily's daughter, Mabel Hancock Latham, and Senator Barry Goldwater, whom she taught when he was a youngster. Her personal reminiscences include clippings of the Hancock home on Cortez Street and their rosewood piano delivered by a team of oxen from Tucson in 1880, the first piano in the Territory. There is also a photo of Mabel, age 4, having her head patted by President Rutherford B. Hayes during his stop at Maricopa train station.

Few personal effects belonging to Lily are included other than a handwritten letter from Los Angeles dated July 23, 1908. Signed by Jennie L. Loving, it comments on Lily's kindness during a recent visit. The letter does not signify if Lily visited Jennie, or vice versa, or the nature of their acquaintance. Did they meet when both were patients at Agnews?

Like many of her female contemporaries, Lily Bell Hancock was a throw-away wife and mother for much of her life, shuttled in and out of the Arizona State Asylum on at least four occasions documented in the State Archives. She also spent time in a comparable facility in California at least twice, as recorded in the Order of May 22, 1904 cited above. Unfortunately, these same papers do not reveal the extent of each stay, the true medical cause, the specific treatment, or the conditions of discharge.

In light of the Hancock family's stature in Phoenix, it could be inferred that Lily was sent away to lessen their embarrassment, together with their hope that she would respond to the treatment and become cured sufficiently to regain what society regarded as acceptable behavior and common sense. To this end, they were willing to expend whatever sums of money were required by the institutions.

Lily Bell Hancock was of hardy stock, surviving until the age of 88 when, on April 27, 1943, she succumbed to pneumonia (terminal congestion of lungs) two months after being hospitalized for a fractured hip. According to the death certificate signed by Leslie R. Kober, M.D. on April 30, 1943, Lily's fall on February 17, 1943 was an accident that occurred in a public place. No details are given, but one would not be surprised if the feisty lady was exerting her independence while out shopping or strolling through the streets of the city her husband had helped create. Following a funeral service conducted by the Very Rev. Edwin S. Lane, dean of Trinity Cathedral, Lily was cremated and interred at Greenwood Memorial Park.

At the time of her death, few if any were alive who remembered that she was among the first Arizona women to inaugurate the Territorial Asylum for the Insane. Her obituary in the April 28, 1943 edition of the Arizona Republic carried no mention of the internal wars that plagued her life or of the family strife that accompanied each passage through those revolving doors. Instead, the column heading blazed: **Mrs. Lily B.**

Hancock, Early Pioneer, Dies.

Lily was a pioneer in more ways than she ever could have imagined the day she and her parents arrived on horseback to begin battle with the Valley's harsh environment. Like many women of her day, Lily fell into an even deeper valley, but while most remained mired beneath its shadow of death and destruction, Lily clawed her way up from its horrors. She lived to see trains, cars, and airplanes surpass the horse and buggy as preferred transportation, and in the pages of a newspaper devoted primarily to the nation's progress in World War II, she earned recognition for her role in history.

Lily Hancock would be even more honored to know that her suffering and the treatments she underwent during the experimental beginnings of clinical psychiatry may have contributed to treatments that today permit many women to conquer depression and other forms of mental stress with outpatient therapy and a single prescription.

Photo of Lillie Bell Hancock circa 1880 courtesy of Arizona State Library Archives

REFERENCES

"Agnew's Insane Asylum," Santa Clara County: California's Historic Silicon Valley, www.nps.gov/history. 3 pages.

Ancestry.com: Arizona Marriage Collection, 1864-1982, Provo, UT.

Ancestry.com: The Kelloggs in the New World, pp. 1520-1529.

Arizona State Library, archives, and Public Records: Territorial Asylum for the Insane, Phoenix, Arizona, Orders of Commitment: Lillie (sic) B. Hancock, March 23, 1886; Lily B. Hancock, May 22, 1904; Lily B. Hancock, July 30, 1906.

Beebe, Lucius. The Central Pacific & The Southern Pacific Railroads. Howell-North Books, Berkeley, California, 1963.

"Capt. William Hancock, Noted Pioneer, Lies in Modest Grave," *Arizona Republic*, April 14, 1942, Section 2, pp. 1, 4.

Certificate of Death of Lily Bell Hancock, Arizona State Department of Health, April 30, 1943.

"Death of Captain W. A. Hancock," *Arizona Republican*, March 25, 1902, p. 8, and March 26, 1902, p. 5.
Edmund T. Wilkins, N.D., "Napa County Biographies," www.calarchives4u.com.

"Judge William A. Hancock," Portrait and Biographical Record of Arizona, pp. 189-193.

"Mrs. Lily B. Hancock, Early Pioneer, Dies," *Arizona Republic*, April 28, 1943.

U.S. Census, Maricopa County, Arizona, 1880, 1900.

"William A. Hancock, Candidate for Surveyor of Maricopa County, for the Independent Party," *Arizona Citizen*, October 10, 1873, p. 3:3.

GRACE VOSS FREDERICK
1905-2009

Grace Caroline Voss came into the world November 20, 1905 destined to cut a vivid swath through American culture directly into the next century. Born in Nepperhan Heights, Yonkers, she was the third child of Reuben Tree Voss, 35 (b. 1870 in New York City) and Olga Rommel Voss, 28 (b. December 25, 1877 in Niagara Falls, New York). Her father, a printer, and her mother, a housewife, knew their daughter was exceptional. She proved them right.

At his print shop in Brooklyn, Reuben Voss published the borough's first "Red Book," the phone directory that set modern

New Yorkers apart from what was still a rural America. His daughter inherited his pioneer spirit toward technology and incorporated it many years later in her masterpiece to man's ingenuity.

Reuben's print shop backed up to the Brooklyn Bridge. When Grace visited him at work in the company of her mother and siblings, the traffic on the mighty span was primarily horses and buggies. Soon she would see those primitive forms of transportation gradually make way for the daring new inventions powered by gasoline motors and driven by dashing young men.

The 1910 U.S. Census finds the family in Westfield, Union County, New Jersey, but the 1920 Census confirms that they had returned to New York and resided in their own home in Queens. By then the three girls, Ruby, 18, Olga, 16 and Grace, 14, had a younger brother Curtis, eight. Helen T. Beckett, age 25, lived with the family, possibly as a housekeeper.

The Voss family lived comfortably in middle-class surroundings. Olga's passport issued May 13, 1922 revealed that the family then resided in Hollis, Long Island, a genteel community in Queens that once was home to former Governor Mario Cuomo and humorist Art Buchwald. Today it is best known as the seat of hip-hop culture.

When Grace Voss lived there, it was but a dream and a subway ride away from Broadway. She had always been an imaginative child, inventing stories and directing her sisters and playmates in plays springing from her fertile mind. At Jamaica High School, her aptitude for drama surged to the fore. Buoyed by encouragement from her teachers, she persuaded her parents to allow her to attend the New York School of Theatre. The school founded by Elizabeth B. Grimball, a greatly admired acting coach, was located at 139 West 56th Street in New York City. There Grace studied in-depth facets of the craft, from the gestures and emotions required for mastery of Shakespeare to fencing and voice projection. She slipped easily into every character demanded of her and firmed her skills by emoting in a variety of roles in many plays.

Her first professional appearances were in vaudeville skits, but it was not long before she caught the attention of important directors while cavorting on those popular stages. Taken by her beauty and talent, many admirers urged her to audition for the legitimate theater, exactly what she had in mind. Her early Broadway run as Kitty Verdun in "Charley's Aunt" was brief. The comedy opened on June 12, 1925 and closed after eight performances. But that did not deter her from developing into a much sought-after leading lady. Each production added to her experience and resumé. In 1927, the attractive blonde starred as Anne Hood in "Her First Affaire." Written by Merrill Rogers and directed by Gustav Blum, the play about a teenager who seduces an older man was daring for its time, perfect for the adventurous Grace. Others in the cast were Stanley Logan, Aline MacMahon and Anderson Lawler.

(Five years later, the play was filmed as a movie in London. It starred the unknown Ida Lupino, then but 19 and a bleached blonde. Her father, the famous comedian Stanley Lupino, traced his show business legacy back to 17th Century Italy. Stanley's wife, actress Connie Emerald, was auditioning for the role of Anne and happened to take Ida along. Instead of casting Connie in the role, as had been expected, the director chose Ida, thus launching another Lupino toward stardom.)

Grace was next cast as "Cinderella," a fairytale role that allowed her to exhibit her ingénue qualities. She thrived on Broadway for the next few years, appearing with fellow thespians Barbara Stanwyck, Spencer Tracy, Basil Rathbone, Tyrone Power and others destined for fame in Hollywood. But a new day was dawning. Ever eager to spread her talented wings, she applied for a position with CBS, a pioneer in broadcasting about to embark on an unproven medium.

During 1931, she appeared on nineteen 15-minute experimental broadcasts, capturing attention with the beauty that enhanced her pantomimes and the perfect enunciation that accented her monologues. Many of the broadcasts were shown at state fairs and public events where crowds gathered to see the novelty that few believed would develop into anything useful. So many thronged into the tents that observation was limited to one minute in order to accommodate all the curious.

Grace was indeed a beauty and so photogenic that her

fabulous face adorned the covers of *Ladies' Home Journal, McCall's*, and other popular magazines during the 1930s. Taking a cue from those experiences, she decided that photography would be a profitable business. It took little coaxing on her part to convince the photographer father of a beau to take her on as an apprentice and teach her the basics. Even before that romance faded, she established herself as a professional photographer and opened her own studio on the top floor of the Theodore Roosevelt Mansion on 57th Street in Manhattan. Her photographs appeared weekly in *The New York Times*. Soon she met amateur photographer Claude Frederick who would become the true love of her life.

    Following their marriage, Grace and Claude plunged into a virgin field, designing theatrical backdrops for the television shows that soon became the daily fare of Americans from coast to coast. The only prerequisite of the scenery and props they created was their ability to withstand lights, action, and live performances. Throughout the 1950s and 1960s, Grace and Claude Frederick were the undisputed brains behind the scenery of major network television shows. They began by providing background stills, but soon created movement with one of their inventions, a three-plex projector capable of projecting nine slides to create a moving effect. The prototype is now on display at Brigham Young University.

To gather props and inspiration for their work, they traveled extensively. Along the way, they amassed rare memorabilia for the dream project tucked away in their hearts: a museum depicting two hundred years of American technological progress. Until their travels took them to Arizona for a vacation at the Sierra Vista dude ranch in Cave Creek north of Phoenix, they had not considered where to construct the museum in their minds.

For several years, they continued to enjoy brief stays at the ranch when their work schedule permitted. Then they learned that a New Jersey physician had purchased the ranch and divided it into 40-acre lots. The option to purchase the pristine property was too good to turn down, especially since Claude's doctor had suggested a change of climate for his health. They had fallen in love with the atmosphere of the town that resembled the western towns recreated on Hollywood lots. Settling for 93 acres of pristine Sonoran Desert, they promptly ordered construction of a mansion they named Hopi House.

When the home was completed in 1973, television's premiere set designers retired, moved to Arizona and turned their attention toward design and construction of the museum. It would occupy the property's air strip once used to ferry local workers to a distant copper mine. Meanwhile, they spread their enormous collection throughout their home and several out buildings. Their regular jaunts to augment Claude's rock collection coincided with Grace's yen for antiques and clothing.

Antique shops had captured her attention from the outset of her career. She continually browsed for potential theatrical costumes and was never happier than when she chanced upon special pieces from eras past to add to her collection. Heeding suggestions from friends and acquaintances or simply following her nose, she traveled great distances to scoop up clothes of all descriptions, some dating back to Martha Washington's time.

Her practiced eye located uniforms from the Civil War, raccoon coats from the 20s, and zoot suits from the WWII period. After moving to Arizona, she acquired dozens of outfits from by-gone days crying out for inclusion in her exhibits.

Among the collection adorning mannequins in the 18,000-square-foot museum are ten bustle dresses from the 1870s, visiting dresses (worn when making polite social calls in the 19th century), livery and bicycling outfits, an early 1800s covered wagon-type dress, a late 1800s maid's uniform, a black widow's dress with veil and parasol worn during the Civil War, a World War II nurse's uniform, ragtime dresses, bordello dresses, flapper dresses, handmade wedding dresses, lingerie, a monkey fur coat, and many others too extensive to list. To entertain local groups, Grace developed a show she called "Streaking Through History with Clothes On." She and friends modeled outfits that encapsulated every decade according to the fashions, history, and music.

When Claude died of cancer in 1981 after a long hospitalization, the museum project might have come to an abrupt halt had not Grace been in charge. The spunky lady, despite her heartbreak, vowed to see their shared dream to completion.

For two decades, all who followed the winding, rocky road past great stands of saguaro were welcomed inside her home to peruse her treasures. On the main level, a glass wall encases a solarium filled with local flora. The view flows outdoors through a sliding door where Grace would strike a gong every evening. Heeding its sound. a deer herd congregated to partake of her treats. They were frequently joined by peccaries, or javelinas, a wild relative of pigs hungry to share in the bountiful feast. Indoors, Grade often retreated to her saloon designed after those standard in the early west for a sip of wine. Later, she might meander into the surrounding rooms to pore over scrapbooks and contemplate cherished mementos of Hollywood films and Broadway.

The lower floor, reached by a circular staircase, which Grace eventually was compelled to master with the help of a cane, was occupied initially by instruments both strange and familiar: phonographs, radios, pianos, jukeboxes, and television sets in every stage of development, even a permanent wave machine resembling a multiple-tentacled Portuguese man-of-war.

An adjacent ranch house was home to dozens of life-like figures positioned in intimate gatherings. Some might have stepped from Godey's fashion book, others from a 19th Century wedding party. Several were assembled around a Chickering grand piano dating back to 1857, once the gift of the Rockefeller family to a Baptist church. Upon completion of the Grace Museum, all were redistributed to their permanent quarters in period-appropriate exhibits.

Every item in the museum is from Grace's personal collection. As far back as the 1930s, she began picking up mementos from shops and skyscrapers being torn down in New York City. She and Claude always returned from their travels with technological oddities that caught their imagination, never exactly certain how they would be utilized, but convinced the opportunity would arise to display them.

A stickler for authenticity, Grace hand-picked Arizona

artist Jason Hoffman to create the murals and backdrops that connect the individual museum exhibits. Together they trace a visual and aural history of American ingenuity. Throughout the final months of preparation, she cruised the length of her museum in a golf cart to make certain that every item in each exhibit passed muster; until her death on January 16, 2009, that golf cart allowed her to delight selected guests in her favorite role of tour guide.

She welcomed Grace Museum visitors into a large atrium, its signature piece a white concert grand piano awaiting the glittering evenings of entertainment she anticipated. It adjoins a theater designed to showcase music and drama groups from local schools and community organizations, as well as professional performers visiting Arizona.

As the tour moved toward the exhibition hall, Grace would pause before the imposing wall of native rock facing the entrance way. It is a striking background for such indigenous creatures as bear, cougar, bobcat, javelina, rabbit, rattlesnake, pack rat, quail, and roadrunner. Grace impressed upon everyone that none that none of the wildlife were intentionally killed for the display; over the past decades, their bodies have been found on or near the property and preserved by taxidermists. An enormous mural covering the adjacent wall silhouettes Native American horsemen framed by a flaming Arizona sunset.

Visitors proceed past exhibits depicting the signing of the Declaration of Independence, the Civil War, the arrival of immigrants to America's shores, the Jazz age, the Great Depression, both World Wars, the Space Age and many other important moments of history. As they pause to observe the scenes, viewers are surprised to behold the figures move and speak, sending shivers up the spine until the hidden technology that brings them to life is revealed by the guide. Each scene resounds with period music and Grace's own distinctive voice narrating the stories, sometimes dramatic, sometimes witty, of past events with links to the present and the future.

Here is the country doctor at the bedside of a young patient felled by one of the diseases man has since eradicated by vaccination. Further along the street, the town barber lures customers to his establishment with a sign broadcasting his fields of expertise: "We Pull Teeth, We Sell Leeches for Blood letting."

The telephone switchboard operator works out of her home, relaying messages along the party line. Ever eager to join in the conversations, she comments on the latest absurd contraption. "You're going to see a moving picture? Who on earth would want to see pictures move?"

While country folk warily adapt to the new technologies, forlorn immigrants pour into Ellis Island. They have survived the passage in the cramped steerage of a great, ocean-going vessel that accommodates aristocrats in luxury on the upper deck. Garbed in top hats and fur coats, those above are unaware of their shabby fellow travelers, some of whom are destined to make their way in the new world as peddlers, trundling their carts through teeming city streets.

Small town families celebrate the Fourth of July on the village square, spreading their picnic baskets before the bandstand while they soak up the sunshine and ditties popular during the early 1900s. Indoors, typical Sunday afternoons are spent in the household parlor, its velvet flocked wallpaper and Oriental rugs reflecting the rise of the middle class. A grandfather clock hovers over the scene as Father reads his newspaper and Mother plays the organ accompanied by Junior on the violin, while Grandmother and Sister marvel at the stereopticon.

Progress meets a brick wall when an irate farmer's wife scolds the driver of a Model T ("Tin Lizzy") for scaring her chickens, but life in post-World War I cities is less rigid. Gangsters and the Jazz Age come to life in a speakeasy where flirty flappers perch on a player piano. The gent strumming a ukulele is updated in the next decade by the Big Band, followed by teens in pony tails and bobby sox dancing around the Wurlitzer jukebox in a 1950s diner, and culminating with Elvis and the arrival of Rock 'n' Roll.

Grace Voss Frederick was young at heart her entire life. A born flirt, she would wink at all the men she encountered at the local post office, taverns, and social gatherings. She loved white wine and unabashedly would savor a glass whenever it was offered. When it was served with a side of her favorite French fries dipped in butter, she became ecstatic.

Her birthdays were cause for celebration throughout Cave Creek. When she reached 95, pilot friends planned special excursions that allowed her to observe from on high the construction of her monument to the country she loved. For the next six years through her 100th birthday, she was treated to jaunts in a bright yellow bi-plane, a hot air balloon, a Huey helicopter and other special aircraft to suit her fancy.

She delighted in living in one of the most scenic parts of America, the Sonoran Desert. Her concern for the environment began many years ago. Shortly after moving to Arizona, she was so outraged to learn of a plan to allow the construction of a mobile home park on a magnificent plot of land that she marched into a meeting of the Maricopa County Supervisors and spoke so eloquently against their plan that the supervisors stood and applauded the feisty little lady who dared waylay their project. Today the road she saved is known as the Desert Foothills Scenic

Drive.

Grace Voss Frederick received many awards during her lifetime, among them the First Women in Communication Award from the Association for Women in Communications. In 2007, she received the Distinguished Patriot Leadership Award from the Sons of the American Revolution. The following year, she was awarded the DAR Medal of Honor from the Daughters of the American Revolution.

Grace maintained her passion for America and its people until the very end at age 103. To all who visited her museum, she exclaimed, "The past 200 years have been the most fascinating time in history. We have progressed from the establishment of this country to technological achievements our forefathers never could have imagined."

Created with love and dedication to historical accuracy, the Grace Museum for the Preservation of Americana is her monument to this nation. Admirers marvel that Grace did not officially begin work on her museum until reaching her 90s. This culminating project of her life is built on a Smithsonian-style scale to echo the determination and work ethic that have touched and inspired the lives of many great people on this planet.

In 2001, she gave 90 acres of her land containing the museum to the Arizona State University Foundation and also donated $6 million to create and maintain a center for cultural improvement. Thanks to Grace's insistence that the land on which it is located be preserved for posterity, the entire collection and the magnificent acres surrounding it will delight generations to come.

A memorial service for Grace was held January 22, 2009 at the Good Shepherd of the Hills Episcopal Church in Cave Creek, Arizona, the western town where the native New Yorker is now a beloved legend.

Grace Voss Frederick, age 94, displays a sassy leg

REFERENCES

"Centenarian keeps past alive in history museum," The Arizona Republic, November 3, 2005, pp. S1, S8.

"Ex-vaudevillian keeps history alive," The Arizona Republic March 31, 2001, pp. 10-11.

"Grace Frederick calls museum of history officially open," Sonoran News, October 1-7, 2003, pp. A1-A2.

Jamai@jamaicahighschool.org.

"Museum makes Graceful Showing," Arizona Highways, November 2002, p. 5.

New York School of the Theatre, Clipping file MWEZ+nc 16,929, Billy Rose Theatre Division, New York Public Library for the Arts.

"Red Mountain Ranch Social Group visits 98-year-old broadcast pioneer," Red Mountain Times, September 2004, pp. 1, 14.

Personal conversations with Grace Voss Frederick, 1998-2008.

FLORENCE JENKINS MUSE
1929-

Florence Jenkins Muse was the seventh of ten children who inhabited the "homeplace," a small frame house at Coles Point, Westmoreland County, Virginia. It backed up to an inlet where the mouth of the Potomac River meets Chesapeake Bay. To most Southerners, the "homeplace" is where they first entered the world and the place where they know they can return throughout their lives to be loved and welcomed, even when the rest of the world casts them aside. Florence's "homeplace" was a metaphor for the mother who raised her and taught her the lessons of caring for others and homespun crafts.

Florence's mother, Ada Elizabeth Pillsbury, was born into a waterman's family so poor they put their girls into domestic service instead of sending them to school. Deprived of formal education, Ada mastered basic household crafts early in life. She learned to clean, polish, cook, and sew so capably that, at the age of 11, she went to work for a family nearby. At 15, she had the good fortune to become employed by a well-to-do family in Washington, DC. While caring for their mansion, she learned about the finer things of life, and upon returning home at 17 to marry Warren Jenkins she vowed to instill those gracious tastes in her own children even as she relied upon God and her ingenuity to made do with the gifts that nature provided.

Her marriage began in a former chicken house made livable by her hands. The centerpiece was a lyre-backed chair purchased for fifty cents. Today that same chair fills the heart of her daughter, Florence, with the music of memories.

Warren, like others in his family, was a waterman. During the winter, he earned his livelihood by plying his small boat around the bay and using a sounding pole to locate the oyster beds. When the oysters were pulled on board by the tongs at the end of the poles, the watermen picked out stones and returned the smaller oysters to the Bay before making their deliveries to the oyster houses. In time, Warren prospered enough to construct a small oyster house adjacent to the "homeplace" where locals shucked the oysters and shipped them to the city.

During the spring and summer, he earned a living by taking wealthy fishing parties onto the Potomac or the Bay. Over the years, he owned three boats, all of them named "Florence" because she shared his love for the water. As a teenager, she often spent summer evenings accompanying her father and brothers in their small boat to gather rock fish from seines operated by a donkey engine. They packed their haul in ice and sent it off to Baltimore.

While Warren and Florence's brothers provided for the family by fishing and hunting, Ada took care of everything else that had to be done for the family. From the time she was a tiny toddler pushing her crab scooter along the sandy bottom of

Machodoc Creek until she left home at 21 to marry her first husband, Florence watched her mother at work and made careful note of the way she prepared the seafood, killed and drew wildfowl, raised baby chickens, made delicious desserts from the abundant fruit in the nearby woodlands, canned the vegetables from the garden she maintained, kneaded dough for bread and biscuits, made beautiful dresses for her daughters without a pattern, and used the scraps for designing lovely quilts. She made lard from the two hogs Warren slaughtered annually by boiling the fat in a kettle. Then she cured the hams and shoulders, pickled the feet, and made gelatin from the heads.

    Once winter set in and the larders were full, Ada found time to treat her family with ice cream made from fresh snow. But when the icy winds brought sickness, her hands made mustard plasters, cold pills from quinine and flour, and herb tea with ginger, lemon, and honey. Because childhood illnesses knew no season, Ada's hands doctored throughout the year making milk and bread poultices for boils and bandages from old sheeting. She burned the tips of needles to kill germs before removing splinters and briars, and applied hot water bottles to earaches.

Ada's sewing basket was both a necessity and a pleasure. When her hands were not mending, altering, and making clothes for the family, she made bedding, crocheted old stockings into rugs, sewed canvas sails for her sons' sailboats, designed necklaces from buttons, or stuffed pillows with fabric scraps. A master at recycling, she impressed upon her children the wisdom of "waste not, want not," a philosophy that gains momentum today among ecology-minded citizens.

No matter the demands upon her every day, Ada set aside time in early morning and late evening to read her Bible and gather strength for the day ahead. Once the Sunday dinner was on the stove, she walked to church armed with lesson plans for her Sunday School class.

The moral and household lessons Ada Pillsbury Jenkins taught by word and deed impacted upon her children, grandchildren, and great-grandchildren. As Florence Jenkins Muse observes, her mother's life, like a pebble thrown into the pond behind the "homeplace," ripples outward and onward from one generation to another.

Florence and her siblings were known locally as "river rats" to the city folks who owned nearby summer cottages. They had but two pairs of shoes, one for school and one for church, so they went barefoot throughout the summer, disregarding pebbles and rocks. They especially loved running through the tall grass catching lightning bugs in a jar as dusk fell.

Florence's sister Nellie was 18 when she went into service as her own mother had done before her. After becoming established with a family in Alexandria, Virginia, Nellie invited Florence to spend three weeks with her during the summer. It was the first trip Florence took away from the Northern Neck and one that she never forgot. Her biggest thrill was tasting her first milkshake and savoring the flavor in her mind until several years later when the scrumptious concoction became available at the local drugstore.

Modern amenities, such as milk shakes, were slow to arrive in the Northern Neck. By the time Florence Jenkins came along, the landscape had changed little since it was visited by Captain John Smith. Many of the flora and fauna that astounded him still flourished, though not in such abundance. The white oak, mulberry, and chinquapin trees host the songbirds while the waterways are rife with swans, cranes, geese and ducks. The woodlands are filled with wild turkeys, raccoons, rabbits, squirrels, opossums, skunks and foxes. Until the bridge was built over the Rappahannock River at Tappahannock, the Northern Neck remained isolated to all but the inhabitants and the wild animals and birds that did not shy away from the resident humans whom they outnumbered. Once visitors discovered the area as an ideal weekend getaway, the creatures became more elusive.

  The rise of affluence in nearby cities and the subsequent influx of weekend sailors had dire consequences for the once-pristine Chesapeake Bay. Algae and red tides began killing the seafood; today the oysters and crabs are depleted and less succulent than old timers remember them.

  Growing up as one of ten children in the home of a

waterman, Florence understood the necessity for hard work. She and her sister learned all the tricks of maintaining a household at their mother's knees while six of their brothers followed their father to the water, forced to go to work by the age of fifteen. Only two of the boys graduated from high school and her sister Nellie was unable to finish school before going to work for the family in Alexandria.

    Florence loved school, but when she graduated at age seventeen, she knew that she was destined to go to work and help her family to the best of her ability. With the offer of a room from friends in Richmond, she boarded a bus to that city in quest of work. Within a few hours, she was hired as a credit department file clerk at the elegant Thalhimer's department store. Two months later, she was so homesick that she returned to Coles Point and began working for Belfield's Country Store. There she cut cheese and sliced bologna for the hungry watermen who anchored their boats in the harbor and she pumped gasoline for the occasional customer who arrived by car.

    At ten dollars a week, a portion of which went to her

parents and the rest to savings, she felt well rewarded, but when business slowed the next summer, the Belfield family could no longer use her services. There was no time to lament the loss of a job because her sister was expecting her third baby. She and her husband begged Florence to stay with them and look after their two older children.

After the baby was born, Florence went to work as a telephone operator for the Tidewater Telephone Company in nearby Warsaw. She enjoyed her work and the opportunity to visit her family in Coles Point often. She might have been happy to make it her career were it not for the call from her former high school principal in early fall. He had always been impressed by her studious attitude. Now he wondered if she would consider becoming a teaching assistant the next semester.

It was exactly what she had dreamed of doing but never dared consider because of the cost of college and time involved. Those problems were solved shortly after she commenced her new job January 1949. When the supervisor dropped around the classroom to observe, she was so impressed that she obtained a scholarship for Florence at Richmond Professional Institute (later renamed Virginia Commonwealth University).

That next September, Florence entered college, moved into the dormitory, and paid for her expenses by working on campus as a switchboard operator and in the mimeograph office. She apportioned her time so well that she was able to complete her studies during the afternoon to leave time for evening socializing. Her bubbly personality made her one of the most popular girls in the dormitory. She was also popular with the men on campus. Even though she had no money for evening gowns when invited to a prom or dance, her friends were happy to share and made certain that she was beautifully attired.

Despite her scholarship and the two jobs, her finances were so limited by the end of her sophomore year that she could not see her way clear to continue her studies. The only way out of the money pit was to return to the telephone company in Warsaw for the summer. After that, the future looked bright because her principal had offered her another position as classroom assistant in the fall. Satisfied with her decision, she accepted one last invitation to visit friends from college and spend the weekend in South Boston, Virginia.

But fate stepped in. Instead of commencing the classroom position in the fall, Florence was thrown into a quandary by a young man she had met during that visit in South Boston. He lived in Richmond and thought nothing of making the journey to Coles Point every weekend to court her. Throughout the summer, he monopolized so much of her free time that she had no opportunity to discuss her doubts with the principal and friends who might have intervened with her best interests at heart.

She later said, "He insisted that it was love at first sight and asked me to marry him so many times that I finally said yes."

That was the first and only time she let another person plan her future. No matter the problems she faced, the decisions she made came from the heart and knowledge that she was doing the best under trying circumstances.

This time, instead of taking the job she truly wanted, she concluded that God had other plans for her. After all, her mother and sister had married young. She was already twenty-one, an advanced age for marriage compared with her family and friends living on the Northern Neck. To prepare for the wedding that she kept telling herself was unwise, she continued at the telephone company and set aside her dreams of making a difference in children's lives.

After their marriage, Florence and her husband moved into a comfortable apartment in Richmond, but she was not content to idle there all day long. Used to being occupied at a useful job, she immediately found a position with the State Planners Bank and Trust Company to utilize her switchboard and clerical skills.

Several months after settling into marriage, she discovered a side to her husband that she had ignored during the courtship. His well-to-do family had spoiled him during his early years and Florence found it difficult to cater to his whims. When he suggested moving to Ft. Lauderdale, Florida to be near his parents, she hoped that would solve some of the problems she encountered trying to deal with him. Instead, the move only exacerbated the problems. She immediately sought work at a local bank and was pleased to receive the same kind of consistent praise she had enjoyed in her past jobs. Each position she held confirmed her belief that learning is a lifetime process and each job you master will prepare you for a new and better challenge.

As the marriage continued to unravel, her husband looked into re-enlisting in the Navy. He had served several years earlier and agreed with Florence that an extended separation would be best for them both. With little fanfare, he sailed away, leaving her to her own devices. Back home she went with scarcely a day to relax before Lloyd Pulley, her former employer at the Tidewater Telephone Company, learned of her arrival and called to ask her to return. She was happy to oblige, but when Mr. Luthy, the principal of Cople High School called to assure her that he had a place for her in the classroom where she belonged, she knew that her prayers truly had been answered.

Florence could not believe her good fortune. Despite her rash decision to marry, the careful plans she once made were falling into place. Now that she and her husband agreed they had leaped into an unfortunate situation, she saw no reason to continue the charade of marriage. Two years after the wedding, she sought a divorce. He did not contest it, convincing her that she was doing the right thing. Despite the breach, she maintained friendly relations with "Mom B.," her former mother-in-law, who continued to welcome Florence into her home whenever she traveled to Florida.

"She told me she would give him up before she would give me up," Florence said. "She lived to be ninety-four and meant the world to me all those years, even though her son and I were no longer together."

Once the divorce was finalized in 1954, Florence wasted no time thinking about her failed marriage. She was in her element in the classroom, hugging and guiding all the children under her charge, sharing her favorite stories and poems, and assuring each that he and she were special. She stinted whenever she could to advance her training. Everything she saved went into tuition. One night a week during the school year, she traveled to Richmond to complete a required course and each summer she took several more so that by 1959 she was a graduating senior.

The degree brought with it not only personal pride, but also a salary boost. Parents were delighted with their children's progress and they responded positively to Florence's individual attention and respect. Most of the students thrived beautifully under her guidance and were ready at year's end to move to the next grade, but a few were immature and unable to grasp the basic concepts as well as their classmates.

Her classes were a joy until an unusually disruptive little girl entered her second grade at the beginning of the term. No matter what approach Florence took, the child kicked and screamed without provocation and bit the other children. It became clear that the reason she did not complete her lessons was her lack of preparation and patience expected of the typical child at age seven. At the close of the term, Florence was sad to fail the girl, but she knew that survival in the third grade would be out of the question for a child unable to master the basics of the second grade curriculum.

When the child took home the report card indicating that

she was not promoted to third grade, her mother became enraged. She flew to the principal and demanded that her daughter be promoted. Not wishing to fuel her wrath, the principal attempted to pacify and assure her that the decision could be overturned. He took Florence aside immediately and insisted that she pass the child to avoid trouble that could echo through the community. To his astonishment, Florence stuck to her principles. Looking the principal in the eye, she told him if the decision meant her job, that would have to be. Her standards did not include compromise in such matters.

The conflict reached the Superintendent of Schools. Patiently, he listened to the principal, Florence, and the parent. After assessing the problem, he sided with Florence and decreed that the child must repeat second grade. The parent was furious and the principal felt betrayed, but Florence profited from her stance. The Superintendent was so impressed by her insight and fortitude that he offered her a position in a new school and gave her an annual raise of a thousand dollars.

Adults and children alike gravitated to Florence. When

she was not spending her weekends being courted by local beaus, she was socializing with the students who adored her and looked to her for support and guidance. One girl in the seventh grade wanted to become a nurse, but poverty and an unhappy home life stood in the way. In her search for a mentor, the girl found one in Florence. The two remained close for many years, traveling around the state together and discovering the many opportunities awaiting one so eager to serve mankind. Florence was proud to attend the girl's graduation from the University of Virginia as a registered nurse, a career that continued to expand and touch on the lives of other young women as she passed along the wisdom and encouragement she received from Florence so many years before.

For five years after her divorce, Florence devoted herself to teaching and the students in her charge. She adored taking those without transportation to the local basketball and baseball games, leading the Methodist Youth Fellowship at the village church, and singing in the choir. Always popular, she had many admirers and went on dates to the movies, games, and festive gatherings, but she did not become serious about anyone until she met Goodwin Muse.

He lived at the other end of the county on a plantation that had been in his family for four centuries. Florence admired his involvement in his church and his community, but was wary about marrying again until she was certain of their compatibility. They dated for a year before she felt certain she was making the right move and could accept the diamond ring he offered repeatedly.

She was wearing it for the first time on Good Friday of 1960. For many years, it had been her custom to attend services on that occasion at the Old Yeocomico Church because the Methodist Church in Coles Point did not have Good Friday services. Instead, she had to forgo church that day because of an illness she had been unable to shake. Once the roads were clear of snow, she made an appointment with a doctor in Richmond. Her sister-in-law volunteered to drive her there, all the better for an enjoyable chat. On their way home along Route 360, they had just entered its crossing with Route 30 when a car barreled through the intersection, ignoring the stop sign, and plowed into them. That car was overturned; theirs was totaled from the front to the back seat.

Her sister-in-law was thrown clear of the wreck, escaping with a back injury and scrapes that sent her home within a week. Florence, however, was thrown from the passenger seat, her left shoulder breaking the steering wheel before she went through the windshield and landed on the hood.

A doctor and his wife, the first to arrive on the scene, agreed, "There is no way she can live."

They did not know Florence and her perseverance. In the hospital, she was wrapped in sheets until Easter Day because of her many broken bones, cuts filled with embedded glass, and her swollen and bruised head. Despite her pain and whispers of dire consequences from the staff and family tip-toeing in and out of her room, she put herself in the hands of the God she had accepted as a "born-again" eight-year-old.

"I bore my cross on Good Friday as my Lord and Savior bore his for the whole world, and by Easter Sunday I knew I would live because I was not bleeding internally," she said.

    She did not know that this was the first of thirty-nine hospitalizations she would endure by the age of 77. But she could only dwell on the future as she married for the second time on August 17, 1960, a few months after her 31st birthday. Following a honeymoon in Niagara Falls, they moved into the beautiful brick home they had built to Florence's specifications on Goodwin's plantation alongside the Potomac River. Florence named it "Brightly." Her inspiration for the name came from her favorite hymn, "How brightly beams the morning star," written during the bubonic plague epidemic by German pastor and composer Philipp Nicolai.

    The Muse's nearest neighbors were the family stationed less than a mile up the road at George Washington Birthplace by the National Park Service to maintain the historical house and surrounding grounds bordering Pope's Creek, an inlet from the Potomac.

    Although she dearly loved the Methodist Church in Coles Point that she had attended since childhood, Florence wanted to please Goodwin and be the best wife possible. Knowing how devoted he had been all his life to the nearby Oak Grove Baptist Church, she joined the church and plunged into every activity possible. She soon was one of the most valuable members, teaching both youth and adult groups and singing in the choir.

During the early years of her marriage to Goodwin Muse, Florence looked forward to February. That is the month when he took a break from farming his plantation and they would travel to Florida for a long, restful stay before planting season began. She loved visiting with her brother Sidney and her former mother-in-law. Both lived there, as did a host of friends who reveled in the warm temperatures.

After the fall harvest, Florence and Goodwin would travel again, often to places she had read about and dreamed of visiting. One of her greatest thrills was arriving at the Mississippi River she knew only from Mark Twain's stories. To firm the experience in her mind, she rode in a steamboat along the waters he once sounded. She paid rapt attention to the levees along the way and the methods used to lower the ships from one level to another so she could describe the procedure to her students.

One fall they traveled to the Herbert Hoover National Monument Park in Iowa to visit their former neighbors, the supervisor and his family who were newly reassigned there following a long tour at the George Washington Memorial Park. They returned by way of St. Louis to contemplate the Gateway Arch, the symbolic beginning of the long, dangerous treks endured by many pioneer families yearning to improve their fortunes in the west. During a trip to Plymouth Rock, she likened the replica of the "Mayflower" to the tiny vessel that brought her ancestors in 1634 to St. Mary's City, Maryland.

"When they came across the water to Coles Point, they saw thick forests, but by 1835 half of the Chesapeake Bay region's forests would be gone from agriculture and timbering," she said. "With the advent of industry along the coast, the pollution from nutrients entering the bay brought red tides causing death and destruction to the fish and wildlife. It took fifteen years for the Chesapeake Bay program launched in 1983 to have any impact. Not until January 2008 did we begin to experience the kind of winters we remember as children with frozen ponds and creeks and snow deep enough to plow."

During summer weekends, Florence and Goodwin entertained friends at picnics on the beach adjacent to their home. While in New England, they heard stories of the Great Sea Serpent that had been observed along the Atlantic seaboard from early days. Florence laughed away the written reports as fancy, not fact, for there was no radio, television or film to corroborate the wild tales told to gullible newspaper reporters by wizened old seamen. It was not until June of 1980 that she changed her mind.

In the company of four friends, Goodwin spotted a creature swimming in the Potomac remarkable for its resemblance to a snake and its length of 10 to 14 feet. As they observed it through binoculars, they based the estimate on the height of the humps surfacing as it swam past their beach.

This was the second such sighting since the summer of 1978 by residents at the mouth of the Potomac. Residents named that beast "Chessie." Zoologists concluded that it was an anaconda descended from South American ancestors accidentally transported years ago in the wooden hulls of commercial sailing vessels. When the ships were left to rot in the Potomac and other estuaries of the Bay, the snakes escaped to roam the Atlantic waters off Virginia.

A sighting off Kent Island, Maryland on May 31, 1982 is the first one documented by electronic age paraphernalia. Robert Frew, a computer salesman, captured the scene on a three-minute color videotape in the presence of house guests whose astonished screams were picked up by the audio. Succumbing to the subsequent media hype and public fervor, Smithsonian zoologist George Zug studied the tape in the hope of answering, once and for all, the burning question: Are sea serpents for real? Florence knows they are.

Between their motor trips across the country and several cruises to the Bahamas, Jamaica and Mexico, Florence underwent three major colon surgeries and a heart blockage. Each time, she bounced back determined to remain available to the students and friends who needed her intervention in problems great and small. Often during the night she would receive a phone call from someone wishing her advice or consolation. She always hurried to the person in need of help and did everything in her power to ease their worry or sorrow.

No matter the occasion, Florence was guided by her love of God and her gratitude for the talents bestowed upon her. Early in 1983, she decided that her devotion could be best shown by celebrating the Lord's birthday in her own way. Thus, she began planning the first of her annual theme-oriented Christmas parties.

"The Lord told me to start simply, so I decided to learn quilting and to use the strawberry as the theme because everyone loves them," she said.

A curious student, as well as a master teacher, she learned new skills rapidly. By Christmas time, she had redecorated and adorned her home with handiwork that included strawberry-covered quilts, draperies, pillows, linens, table arrangements, and a menu inspired by the luscious fruit. For good measure, she discovered china and glassware in local shops to blend perfectly with the theme.

The party was such a hit that she began planning an

Apple Christmas 1984 before the last guest departed. By midwinter, Florence was exploring local church sales, antique shops, and novelty stores for objects and material destined to represent apples or apple trees. During her search, she could not ignore the straw hats, potpourris, milk pails, and crisp gingham begging to become part of her Country Christmas 1985.

    Over a lifetime, Florence gathered what some have called the largest private shell collection in the country. Displayed in the glass encased cabinet of her guest room, they were a natural theme for Christmas 1986. Guests that year marveled at yards of handiwork delicately embroidered with shells, striking nautical arrangements tucked into every nook of her home, and a menu created around succulent seafood dishes served, quite naturally, in shells.

    Christmas 1987 celebrated the Songs of Christmas, beginning with the strains of "Jingle Bells" resounding from a red sleigh manned by Santa in the front yard. "Frosty the Snowman" ushered guests past the portico to the front door where a tape recorder playing "White Christmas" was camouflaged by a sparkling white wreath.

Indoors, chimes played "Silent Night" alongside the manger scene. The hallway ceiling decked with thick boughs of holly and mistletoe, accompanied by a chorus of "Deck the Halls," pointed the way to the living room dominated by an enormous Christmas tree decorated as early German settlers might have envisioned "O Tannenbaum."

Wherever one wandered throughout the house, Christmas music poured from every room and cranny, here a snow-covered village representing "O Little Town of Bethlehem," there a squadron of heavenly hosts caroling "Hark! The Herald Angels Sing," even a trio of Dickensian figures cavorting atop the bathroom vanity warbling "God Rest Ye Merry, Gentlemen."

While guests exclaimed in delight, Florence ferried delectables from the kitchen to the buffet, a menu inspired by Merrie Olde England. Her silver tray was heaped with roast beef that was carved and stuffed into hot rolls or mated with Yorkshire pudding. It was flanked by potted cheese, plum puddings, trifles, currant cakes, mincemeat pies, and platters of coconut cookies made from Florence's secret recipe.

For her Victorian Christmas of 1988, she transformed her home into a satin-and-lace turn-of-the-century dwelling sparkling with cut-glass hurricane lamps and bowls. Bisque-headed dolls lolled lazily in wee rocking chairs, and the Christmas tree fairly dripped with dainty ornaments of feathers, lace, and cut-paper. The menu, adapted from one served by a noted tycoon, consisted of baked Virginia ham and biscuits, roasted oysters, clam chowder, fruit pies, a variety of layer cakes, and immense bowls of fruit.

A Children's Christmas of 1989 honored the growing number of children in the wide circle of Florence's family and friends. A life-size bear in the outdoor sleigh greeted arriving guests. Indoors, fifty-two huggable teddy bears, all wearing Santa hats fashioned by Florence, were stationed throughout. Each went home with a happy tot, who also "shopped' for two gifts from the guest room toy store.

Early American décor throughout the house included a Log Cabin quilt Florence made for the occasion, fresh new wallpaper hung with her usual swish, and handmade rag rugs throughout in shades of blue with red and white accents. The Christmas tree was draped with popcorn strings and tiny, fuzzy animals. On the stove, cauldrons bubbled with taffy the youngsters pulled after consuming their fill of hamburgers, hot dogs, baked beans, coleslaw, potato salad, chocolate chip cookies, and homemade ice cream.

Could Florence top this? Just ask the guests who attended her White Christmas of 1990, followed by Christmas With Nature in 1991. At the latter, guests went home with favors of mini-market baskets Florence learned to make in a basket-weaving class. After dying the finished baskets in solutions of coffee and tea to achieve rustic coloring, she filled them with brown eggs purchased from a local chicken farmer. The tree ornaments were birds' nests holding eggs. The tree itself was wrapped with grapevine.

A Christmas Tree Christmas in 1992 featured a decorated tree in every room of the house, each distinctive from the others. The menu included desserts of cookies, cakes, and pies all shaped like pine trees. The theme in 1993 was the Good Old Days, allowing Florence to rekindle memories with the homey contraptions and favorite foods remembered from childhood. A nativity set made by her nephew Sammy was the buffet centerpiece for The First Christmas of 1994. From greens, she fashioned palm trees to emulate those indigenous to the Holy Land.

Because of Goodwin's failing health, Florence decided that 1995 would be the final big Christmas celebration at Brightly. To charm children and adults alike, she decided on a theme of Mr. and Mrs. Santa Claus, represented by a jolly couple dressed for the occasion. After Mrs. Claus greeted the guests entering the large family room, Santa arrived with an enormous bag of toys filled with ample gifts for every child present. It was a joyous and fitting way to conclude the beloved tradition.

Florence's gala Christmas parties brought together a congenial, yet eclectic, assemblage of kinfolk, church members, neighbors, the National Park Service staff, former students, local farmers, teachers, the Westmoreland County Garden Club, and friends from distant corners of the state. Touched by their hostess's empathy, enthusiasm for life, and year-long devotion to the Lord's birthday, they cherish memories of those special holidays.

All the while she was tending to Brightly, holding forth in the church, and planning her extravagant Christmas celebrations, Florence was teaching. Although her increased responsibilities after marriage eventually necessitated leaving the regular classroom, she could not desert the children who needed her. She finally compromised by working three mornings each week with homebound, special needs children. They are the subjects of her book, <u>These Are My Children</u>.

"Persons with dyslexia are very intelligent individuals," she said. "Teaching them simply takes the right approach. I've worked with dyslexic students for more than 50 years and know that the visual image one sees reflects backwards as a mirror image on the brain. Naturally, it's almost impossible for them to master reading and language skills."

To accommodate their handicap, Florence developed a

tactile teaching method. She began by writing the word, letter, or number correctly on the student's back. She then expanded the process by using letters and numbers made of sandpaper and having students write on velvet or corduroy pillows. Early on, it became clear to her that the methods she employed enabled those who were dyslexic to develop their personalities, verbal and communication skills, memory, and self-confidence. In fact, her program works so well that young students can advance several grade levels in reading in a short time. She points out that the younger they are, the quicker the condition can be alleviated and the sooner the student can progress to the level of peers.

Florence taught many dyslexics who compensated for their problem with exceptional memories. As they grow older, many use alternate communication skills so well that their handicap cannot be detected. She found that those who do not hide their handicap are a joy to be around. However, she warned that those who are not treated and hide it can develop three harmful characteristics:

* Controlling people and the environment around them,

* Becoming masters of deception, and

* Twisting the truth and/or lying. If properly taught, dyslexics can turn the tendency to control into profitable leadership. If not, they are very difficult to be around. Some dyslexics can lead two or three lives at the same time without being detected.

Over the years, Florence kept mementos and notes about every child she taught. Here follow several excerpts about children who touched her life.

<u>Rick</u>. Rick's mother brought him to my home when he was a young student because he was having difficulty learning in school. One of the causes was a hearing difficulty. He was shy and very serious. Today he is president and co-owner of his family business which began small and grew into a corporation.

<u>Mark and Ruth</u>. Mark and Ruth were teenagers when they moved with their family to our community from Utah. They were very good students except for the fact that in Utah they were not taught English grammar. They had not heard of diagramming a

sentence; nor were adverbs, gerunds, etc. part of their vocabulary. I began tutoring them after school and they soon were doing fine. Both attended college, married and had lovely families. We remain close friends and, after my husband's death, they became guardians to me.

<u>Jessica</u>. Jessica was born with a serious eye disease and a radiant personality. As my second grader, she had thick glasses and a brilliant mind that soaked up knowledge like a sponge. When she became high school age she was blind and could no longer go to school, so I became her tutor. While tutoring her for two years, I let her family know what an advantage she would have by going to the School for the Deaf and Blind where she would learn Braille. They finally consented and Jessica went on with her happy, busy life. She married and had a son and recently attended her alumni banquet to celebrate 39 years since graduation. She does volunteer work and goes to a resort for the blind on weekends for recreation. Jessica writes, "Life just keeps getting better."

Nelson. Nelson was a junior high teenager who had become so undisciplined that he began showing up in juvenile court. His father asked me to help his son. When Nelson first came to my door, I told him, "I will not think of your past. Today you begin with a clean sheet of paper. If a black mark goes on that paper, you will put it there. I told him that whatever he told me would be in complete confidence unless he did something that risked his life or that of someone else. Then I would have to tell his dad.

"I never broke my promise until Nelson began hanging out at a beer parlor where stabbing and shooting took place. Fearful for his life, I had to tell his dad. At first Nelson was very mad at me, but he soon realized I had done it for his own good. After that, we had many good times together. He became interested in playing a guitar, so I gave him one I seldom used. He also began walking along the beach with a metal detector or "bounty hunter" looking for treasure. I had recently bought a new one from my brother, so I let him have it for half price knowing that God wanted me to devote my life and possessions to finding the "treasure" in children.

"When Nelson reached high school, he went to a church-related Boys Ranch and Academy in Oklahoma. There he joined the Boys' Choir that traveled around the country singing in churches. While my husband was ill, Nelson came from Oklahoma with his wife and children to see me. The treasure we have together is a special love for each other.

Marshall. Marshall was from one of the islands in the Chesapeake Bay. He came to live in our community because his father was a waterman. He dropped out of seventh grade, but I hated to see him not have an education, so his parents agreed to let me tutor him and give him exams so he could enroll in high school. He graduated from high school and went into the Air Force to further his education. We kept in close touch as he rose in rank, married, and had a nice family. It gives me great joy to know I helped this young lad make a real difference in his life.

Frank and Lee. Frank, 8, had a "lazy tongue" caused by the frenulum, a small fold of mucous membrane from the floor of the mouth to the middle of the underside of the tongue. His extended too far toward the front of the tongue. Sometimes it is clipped, but that may not solve the problem. Before I left his home that first day, it was clear to me that his brother Lee, 14, had the same problem. It was also evident that Lee faced far more ridicule in junior high with his problem than did Frank. Peers are important, so I could not go to the home to tutor one boy and not the other. Within a year, Lee was recording "The Gettysburg Address" for me. His teachers could not believe how I helped him. Today he has a lovely wife and son, a fine job, and plays a guitar with a local band. Frank also learned to speak well and, when the school finally hired a speech therapist, Frank told her she ought to get Mrs. Muse to teach her how to teach speech therapy. His mother had a good laugh from that comment.

Jean. Jean was a shy, little girl needing speech therapy for a "lazy tongue" syndrome. Today she works at the drive-in window of my local bank and greets everyone with a confident, "How are you doing?"

<u>Jean Pierre</u>. Jean Pierre had the most severe speech problem I encountered. Some of the best speech pathologists in Richmond had worked with him, but they were using the wrong method. On the first day of tutoring, he said to me, "Mrs. Muse, if you give me the tools to speak, I will work with them."

A mirror is a valuable tool in teaching correct speech. As the child watches the teacher say the letters and words correctly, he/she can see how it is done and then practices in the mirror. By the end of the summer his father thought he was speaking with his little girl on the phone instead of his little boy. Today my "little Frenchman" is a handsome grown man employed with a men's clothing store in one of Richmond's popular shopping malls.

Florence's love for her many children was returned tenfold. A letter from one student dated November 16, 2004 reflects the feelings of those who soared to new heights under her tutelage.

"My Dearest Mrs. Muse,

Many years ago, God sent me an Angel.

This Angel took her hands and with tender belief in me, began to write letters on my back; she showed me that I wasn't stupid but very special. My Angel taught me elementary things very differently. With the love in her heart and guidance from God, my Angel began to rebuild this little girl, to give back to her a belief that she could do anything.

Today this little girl is a grown woman. The Angel is always in her thoughts and heart. When I begin to doubt myself, God takes me back to a precious time in my life to remind me I can do anything!

With all my Love,

Christine.

While Florence taught, she prudently saved a portion of her salary. After her marriage, she saved much more because Goodwin paid the major bills. However, as time caught up with him, he became very evasive and she began to fear that his mind was going. He began questioning her about every purchase, and when she wore a new item of clothing, he insisted knowing where it came from and how much it cost. As he became more and more belligerent about her spending any money whatsoever on herself, she found it best to pay for her clothes out of her own funds to avoid an argument.

It was not long before she was convinced that it was imperative for her to save nearly everything she earned from teaching and squirrel it away unbeknown to Goodwin. The less he knew, the better. Several years before his death, she concluded that she had much to fear. Almost daily he raved about expenses or anything else that irked him. He had always been secretive about his financial situation. That had not bothered her at the outset of their marriage when he cheerfully funded their trips, her elaborate parties, and anything else she desired. Now their discussions inevitably ended with him shouting about her transgressions that existed in his mind alone.

At last she discovered the awful truth: by tradition, the

Muse plantation is passed from son to son. It was originally settled in mid-to late 1600s by John Muse at the point where Popes Creek meets the Potomac River. Although a portion of the original property is now George Washington's Birthplace owned by the National Park Service, the remainder is recognized as the oldest American farm still under continual ownership by the founding family. In keeping with the Muse family tradition that has continued from the English immigrant to this day, the farm is passed on to the next male Muse in line. Upon the death of the owner, the land is immediately taken over by the intended recipient. The most shocking stipulation is that Muse wives do not inherit the property or any part of it and are summarily evicted.

According to the tradition that had been passed down for four centuries, when Goodwin died on December 2, 1999, Florence Jenkins Muse was obliged to leave "Brightly." At once. Having suspected the worst for some time, she salted away every dollar that came her way. To her joy, the "homeplace" at Coles Point came on the market about the time Goodwin's health began a steady decline. She had by then accumulated enough for a modest down-payment and gambled that she would one day be able to purchase it outright. Because the house was in disrepair, she managed to convince the owner to reduce the price and came away from the deal elated for the first time in many years.

Faced with urgency, she began traveling back and forth regularly to refurbish it. First came days of scrubbing, followed by applications of fresh paint and wallpaper. As the restoration progressed, she added attractive window treatments and braided rugs. Local laborers completed basic repairs inside and cut back the wild overgrowth in the yard until the 300 year-old fig tree, the elderly azaleas, and gnarled crape myrtles once more prevailed above the neat lawn. When Goodwin's nephew arrived after the funeral to claim "Brightly" for his own, Florence was ready to depart with a local moving van poised to transport her beloved belongings to the house where she was born.

On January 5, 2009, ten years after Goodwin's death, Florence celebrated 60 years of teaching at a festive occasion attended by former students and faculty. At that time, she mused about the memories ferrying her back to yesteryear.

"I don't know who was the happiest to be back at school, the students or this old teacher who loves to be with them weekday mornings," she said. "Besides just showing their love and appreciation for me, they make me feel young. Many grown-ups don't do that quite as often as they should these days.

"Why do they call these the Golden Days? The things we did long ago seem so clear, and yet we can't remember where we put our coat when we came in the door.... One great gift we are given as we get older is Wisdom. Reminds me of the young boy who at sixteen thought his father was dumb, but at the age of twenty-one, he asked his father, 'How did you learn so much in just five years?'

"Years give us lots of sorrow and pain, but years also give us wisdom and we can help many along the way by sharing it with our fellow man. Don't let age with its problems and pain blur the gift of wisdom that God has imparted to you along the way. After all, we will not pass this way again."

Florence Jenkins Muse with two of her beloved students

REFERENCES

Muse, Florence Jenkins. <u>My Mother's Hands: A Biography of Ada Elizabeth Pillsbury Jenkins</u>. Self-published, 2004.

Muse, Florence Jenkins. <u>These are My Children: A Teacher's Notebook.</u> Self-published, 2005.

Muse, Florence Jenkins. <u>Travel With Me.</u> Self-published, 2008.

Conversations with Florence Jenkins Muse from 1985-2009.

Audacious American Women

Made in the USA
San Bernardino, CA
09 February 2013